To Cyn'
Ceou ...
Ro. 8:28

Hidden in His Hands

Held by His Heart

Bishop Carlos L. Malone, Sr

Love of Peace

Bishop Carlos L. Malone Jr.

Phil. 4:13

6-13-97

Hidden in His Hands

Held by His Heart

Bishop Carlos L. Malone, Sr.

Take note that the name satan and related names are not capitalized. We choose not to acknowledge him, even to the point of violating grammatical rules.

Treasure House

An Imprint of
Destiny Image® **Publishers, Inc.**
P.O. Box 310
Shippensburg, PA 17257-0310

"For where your treasure is
there will your heart be also." Matthew 6:21

ISBN 1-56043-274-8

For Worldwide Distribution
Printed in the U.S.A.

Treasure House books are available through these fine distributors outside the United States:

Christian Growth, Inc.
Jalan Kilang-Timor, Singapore 0315

Successful Christian Living
Capetown, Rep. of South Africa

Omega Distributors
Ponsonby, Auckland, New Zealand

Vine Christian Centre
Mid Glamorgan, Wales, United Kingdom

Rhema Ministries Trading
Randburg, Rep. of South Africa

WA Buchanan Company
Geebung, Queensland, Australia

Salvation Book Centre
Petaling, Jaya, Malaysia

Word Alive
Niverville, Manitoba, Canada

This book and all other Destiny Image
and Treasure House books
are available at Christian bookstores everywhere.

Call for a bookstore nearest you.
1-800-722-6774
Or reach us on the Internet: **http://www.reapernet.com**

Dedication

This book is dedicated first of all to God, my heavenly Father; Jesus Christ, my personal Savior; and the Holy Spirit, my paraclete and comforter.

To my wife Pamela, who for 15 years has been by my side growing with me and growing in her understanding of what God has called me into. I thank her for her commitment to her roles of wife, mother, and friend. The depth of my love for her is a book all by itself. Pamela, I love you very much.

To three of the greatest children that any parent could ever ask for, Ashley, Andrea, and Carlos, Jr. You are the lights of my life. May my life be a light for you.

To my parents, Roosevelt and Mary Malone, thank you for raising me the way that you did. Thank you for your discipline, direction, and dedication to seeing to it that my brothers, sisters, and I understood what it meant to be honest and live godly lives. Wherever or however we have failed, it was not because of you. If I had to be born again in the natural sense, I would still want you as my parents. I love you dearly.

To my six brothers, Rick; Kevin; Roosevelt, Jr.; Roderick; Steve; and Jarrod; and to my three sisters, Veronica, Carmen, and Genyne, I also dedicate this book to you. May you find within its contents a source of both power and purpose that you may always know whose hand is really keeping you. I love you.

To my godson, Raye, whose feet and hands have been anointed of God to bring praise and glory to Him through the art of dance. May the hand of the Lord continue to guide you and the Vessels of Praise liturgical dance ministry. I love you as if you were my natural son.

Finally to my church family, Bethel Baptist Church, the support that you have given to me, my family, and my ministry, is deserving of an Academy Award. The ministry success that we have achieved, we attribute to your "followship." Thank you for your continual encouragement in all of my many endeavors. My love for you will always be displayed within my commitment to teaching you the whole Word of God without compromise. I will always strive to carry myself in a way that will not embarrass you. Let's stay together because we're going somewhere.

Contents

Foreword

I remember sitting in a homiletics class and para-phrasing a definition of *anthropomorphism*. I said it was: "God revealing himself in language man can understand; God talking man-talk." Under the guidance of the Holy Spirit, Bishop Carlos Malone has delivered to the reader an anthropomorphic masterpiece. His blend of interpre-tation, illustration, and application shows us the hand of God. Like taking off a glove, Bishop Malone has exposed the glory of God in a manner that helps the reader visu-alize the presence of the hand of God in his or her life. This work is a rare and refreshing literary synthesis of practicality and spirituality. Bishop Malone has success-fully achieved the challenging goal of presenting the per-sonhood of God in both theological and practical images.

One of the challenges in the ministry of the Word is to maintain a balance between textual integrity and prac-tical insight. The presentation of incomprehensible con-cepts of an infinite God in terms comprehensible to finite man is the mountain that every dedicated pulpiteer faces weekly. Bishop Malone has climbed that mountain, stood on the pinnacle of homiletical excellence, and proclaimed the good news of a God who is not only transcendent but also imminient. This portrait of the hand of God speaks of the proximity of a Divine Father who is interested and involved in the lives of His children. This writer helps us realize the sensitivity and compassion of our loving God by spotlighting His ability to reach down into the realities of our lives with a hand of provision, protection, and power.

Bishop Malone's flowing style first captures you; then it carries you into a revelation of the caring God who makes Himself available to the humanity He sent His Son to save. With exact exposition and authentic application Bishop Malone shows us the multifaceted nature of God: He humbles us under God's hand of mercy. He sustains our hearts by God's hand of keeping power. He encourages us with God's hand of blessing. He helps us understand God's hand of deliverance. He gives us hope with God's hand of healing. He corrects us with God's hand of discipline. He confronts us with God's hand of judgment. He directs us with God's hand of guidance, and he inspires us with God's hand of assurance.

May you be blessed as you see the hand of God in your life.

Kenneth C. Ulmer, Ph.D.
Bishop of Christian Education
Full Gospel Baptist Church Fellowship

Prologue

Throughout the Bible are many references to the hand of God. Persons used powerfully by God spoke reverently of the hand of God—some even claiming to have seen an actual physical manifestation of His hand.

The hand of God. What is it? Is it simply God's provision for His children, or is it something more?

The prophet Ezekiel wrote:

And it came to pass...as I sat in mine house, and the elders of Judah sat before me, that the hand of the Lord God fell there upon me. Then I beheld, and lo a likeness as the appearance of fire: from the appearance of His loins even downward, fire; and from His loins even upward, as the appearance of brightness, as the colour of amber. And he put forth the form of an hand, and took me by a lock of mine head; and the spirit lifted me up between the earth and the heaven, and brought me in the visions of God to Jerusalem…And, behold, the glory of the God of Israel was there, according to the vision that I saw in the plain (Ezekiel 8:1-4).

In Luke, we see that the people of Israel perceived that the hand of the Lord was upon Jesus while He was yet a child (Lk. 1:66).

In Joshua, we read the account of how the Lord dried up the river Jordan, just like He parted the Red Sea, so the Israelites could cross it, "That all the people of the earth might know the *hand of the Lord*, that it is mighty: that ye might fear the Lord your God for ever (Josh. 4:24).

First Samuel contains the story of God's dealings with the idolatrous people of Ashdod, whose worship of the pagan god Dagon was an affront to God: "But the *hand of the Lord* was heavy upon them of Ashdod, and He destroyed them, and smote them with emerods, even Ashdod and the coasts thereof" (1 Sam. 5:6).

In First Chronicles, Jabez called on God, saying, "…Oh that Thou wouldest bless me indeed, and enlarge my coast, and that Thine hand might be with me, and that Thou wouldest keep me from evil, that it may not grieve me! And God granted him that which he requested" (1 Chron. 4:10).

The hand of God is the same hand that created heaven and earth. It's the same hand that reached down from heaven to save mankind from sin and death. It is the same hand that rested upon David when he slew Goliath. It's the same hand that guides us through danger, both seen and unseen. The hand of God is a powerful hand, an omnipotent hand.

Blessings, provision, gifts, callings, enablement, deliverance, chastisement, judgment, guidance, assurance; all these things and more are attributes of the hand of God. As you continue in this study of the hand of God, which was given to me by the inspiration of the Holy Spirit, may the eyes of your understanding be opened to the necessity and value of walking intimately before God with His hand upon you daily. May you receive insight and revelation knowledge from these pages.

1

God's Hand of Mercy

A nd Satan stood up against Israel, and provoked David to number Israel. And David
said to Joab and to the rulers of the people,
Go, number Israel from Beersheba even to Dan; and
bring the number of them to me, that I may know it.
And Joab answered, The Lord make His people an
hundred times so many more as they be: but, my lord
the king, are they not all my lord's servants? why
then doth my lord require this thing? why will he be
a cause of trespass to Israel? Nevertheless the king's
word prevailed against Joab. Wherefore Joab departed, and went throughout all Israel, and came to
Jerusalem. And Joab gave the sum of the number of
the people unto David. And all they of Israel were a
thousand thousand and an hundred thousand men
that drew sword: and Judah was four hundred three-
score and ten thousand men that drew sword. But Levi

and Benjamin counted he not among them: for the king's word was abominable to Joab. And God was displeased with this thing; therefore He smote Israel (1 Chronicles 21:1-7).

When the merciful hand of God is upon a person's life, it seems all that he does will blossom and bloom; whatever he does is blessed by God. Is it because that man or woman is particularly righteous or especially deserving? Or is it a matter of God's poured out grace—His mercies that are new every morning (see Lam. 3:22-23)?

David, king of Israel, was described as "a man after God's own heart" (see 1 Sam. 13:14). Yet he was at times disobedient and displeased God. One instance is described in First Chronicles; David tempted God by sending Joab throughout the land of Israel to perform a census among the people. Here was a man who had submitted his life to God. He had experienced miracles of might and valor. He had prevailed against a jealous Saul to ascend to the throne of Israel. Now he was resorting to trusting in flesh, not God.

And God was displeased.

When you give yourself over to the Lord, you are in His hand. His hand comes upon you, and you become overshadowed by Him. From this point forward, "Greater is He that is in you, than he that is in the world" (1 Jn. 4:4b). He is the Greater One, and He is in charge.

I don't care what the situation may look like. I don't care how ghostly or spooky things may appear. I don't care how evil the adversary may seem, or how insurmountable the circumstances—if God is for you, who can be against you? (See Romans 8:31.) You should have confidence in that. In fact, there should never be a time in your life when you should even have to question that fact or think about how things are going to work out, not when God's hand is on you. As long as His hand is upon you, you should know that everything is going to be all right.

Yet there is confusion about the presence of the hand of God. Some people think God has put His hand upon them because of who they are. They think God has placed His anointing upon them because of who they are. However, it's not because of who you are; *it's because of who He is!* He's a gracious God, a merciful God, and because of His grace—not your worthiness—He puts His hand upon you.

The grace of God—the favor of God—is unmerited favor; unconditional favor; favor not based upon your worth, but upon your faith in the ability of God. It is by your faith and out of His faith that you can enter into covenant relationship with Him. And it is possible to start out right, with everything going along God's way, then get sidetracked somehow. That's what happened when David gave Joab the royal orders to number Israel.

What Went Wrong With David?

Here was a great king, a man who obviously loved God...but who was also a fallen man with many faults. He was an adulterer and a murderer. He schemed. He plotted. He got into the flesh, not once, but often. Yet of David, God said, "He's a man after My own heart!"

If there is a lesson here, it's this: Just because you get promoted in life, don't become so caught up with where you are that you think only good things are going to happen to you. When you become blinded by the success you worked so hard to achieve, you are most vulnerable to the enemy. And in case you think the good things happening to you are in some way due to how much you pray, how far you've come, or your position with the Lord, think again. It's not about you or what you do or don't do; it's about the Lord. He is the reason you have had victories. He is the reason you have received what you have today.

Every battle you've gone through, He won for you. I don't care if He did supply all the necessary weapons of your warfare. It is still God who gives the victory. So don't ever try to measure your success by your own measuring rod. Never read your own press clippings. Never let people pump you up into thinking you are greater than you are, because in the midst of it all is the hand of God.

The hand of the Lord was upon David's life. He had known many victories through the power of God's might. Yet he tempted God by endeavoring to number his kingdom—count heads, so to speak, as if to admire what his own flesh had done.

God was displeased, the Scripture says.

It was God who won those victories through David and the men of Israel. It was *not by might, nor by power* but by the Spirit of the living God (see Zech. 4:6).

It's not about me. It's not about you. It's not about David, king of Israel. *It's about God.*

Once you understand that it's not about you—your giftings, your anointing, your ability, your personality, your talent, your family, your reputation, your status, your money, your specialness—you have the key to the principle of prosperity. Many people can sing, but not many have national recording contracts. It's not talent; it's the anointing of God, His favor, His hand.

Failure to understand that simple thing is why so many people become frustrated. They think, *I can sing as well as she can. Why does she get all the solos?* Or perhaps they think, *I can preach as well as he can. Why does he get to do all the preaching?*

Why? Because it's not your season to sing. It's not your season to preach. It's not about how good you can sing or preach; it's about God. Stop thinking that things are bound to come together in a certain way because of you—and who you are. Things don't work together for good because of who you are; they work together for good for them that love God (see Rom. 8:28). It is not because of talent, not because of ability, but because of God, and our love for Him. It's about God, not about you!

It's about the anointing, the hand of the Lord. When His hand rests upon a person, he or she may be the most untalented person there is yet wind up being used in powerful and unusual ways. The person whose voice is not very good, when anointed by God may sing so sweetly that he or she comes to the attention of the right person in the record business—who gives that person a recording contract! Or it may not go that way at all. But with God, nothing is impossible. All things are possible, because of Him...not you!

You may think, *It's because of my personality! That's why I'm a success!* This is not necessarily true. Your personality without His power is a legacy. The principle is similar to the operation of a battery. You don't connect a positive battery terminal to another positive one. You match a positive with a negative. When your "negative" connects with God's "positive," that's when the anointing starts to flow—positive to negative. When the connection is right, you get power!

Without God, we are nothing. When our nothingness connects with His somethingness, the power of God is released. That's what makes the difference.

David Forgot...

Verse 1 of First Chronicles 21 explains that the devil provoked David to number Israel. David had forgotten God's power and thus was made vulnerable to the enemy's tactics. Don't ever say, "The devil made me do it!" He has no power to make you do or say anything. Don't say, "The devil made me...." Say, "I let the devil...." That's what David did; He forgot God and let the devil in.

If you want to kill the whole body, first kill the head. That's how it's been done in warfare for centuries. Head wounds are the worst, and they are usually fatal. You may hear of every type of organ transplant, from heart to lungs to liver and even of several organs transplanted at once. But you won't hear of a "head transplant." Without your head you're a goner. You may have the strongest heart there is, the best liver and kidneys; but without your brain you're in trouble. When the brain dies, you die.

Thus, if satan cuts off the head, the whole body dies. The devil wanted to destroy all Israel, so he went after David—the head.

That is why it is so important that the person God has placed over your soul should not be the topic of your gossip, but your prayers.

Having placed David over Israel and anointed him to be king, God stood back and watched how he dealt with all that power. Then came satan, ready to entice him. He didn't come in boldly and suggest, "David, why not number Israel?" No, he eased up on the king and began to move him slowly toward where he wanted him. He whispered, "David, you know you're a bad dude! Remember when all the women of Israel were making such a fuss over you? They cried out that Saul had killed his thousands but you had killed tens of thousands. You're bad! You've got all these thousands out there fighting for you. How many soldiers was that? You're winning all these battles because you have...how many men do you have enlisted in your army?"

David forgot God and began to listen to the enemy.

Big mistake! The devil's a liar.

Many people who begin the right way fall by the wayside because they let the devil lie to them by massaging their big egos. The devil will say anything to get a man or woman of God off track. He'll work on their egos until they eventually succumb.

That's what happened to David. The devil enticed him, and David bit the bait.

There are some things we just don't need to know. David didn't need to know how many men were fighting for him. He was God's man, answerable directly to Him. The hand of the Lord was upon him. But David became caught up in his own importance and went on an ego trip. He may have marveled at how smart he was. He may have desired to feel even more important, so he gave the order to Joab to number Israel. But what difference did it make? David hadn't won those battles because of how many troops he took against the enemy; he won because of the hand of the Lord.

Joab sensed God would not look favorably on this act. He warned David that it wouldn't make any difference to know the number. Nevertheless, he went forth and did as the king had commanded.

Numbers didn't mean anything to Israel. Here was a land with a mighty track record of faith—the land of Gideon, whose own troops were decreased by God until just he and a small band of men defeated a giant foe. God—the great God of multiplication—had proven time and again that numbers didn't mean anything because of

His ability to take that which is small and insignificant and make it great and mighty.

Joab said, in effect, "David, why take this census, since you already have the victory? It's not a numbers game, David; it's about God. Do you want to anger Him?"

But Joab did as he was told because, after all, David was the king. He didn't like it, but he began to count. And when he got to the tribes of Levi and Benjamin, Joab stopped counting. Then watch what happened in verse 7:

> *And God was displeased with this thing; therefore He smote Israel. And David said unto God, I have sinned greatly, because I have done this thing: but now, I beseech Thee, do away the iniquity of Thy servant; for I have done very foolishly* (1 Chronicles 21:7-8).

There—he saw it! "I was a fool—just for a minute. I became my own counsel, my own audience, my own cheerleader, and I forgot You!"

At last, David had seen the truth. He had listened to the devil, but in repentance he begged God, "Deal with me!"

> *And the Lord spake unto Gad, David's seer, saying, Go and tell David, saying, Thus saith the Lord, I offer thee three things: choose thee one of them, that I may do it unto thee. So Gad came to David, and said unto him, Thus saith the Lord, Choose thee either three years' famine; or three months to be destroyed before thy foes, while that the sword of thine enemies overtaketh thee; or else three days the sword of the Lord, even the pestilence, in*

the land, and the angel of the Lord destroying throughout all the coasts of Israel. Now therefore advise thyself what word I shall bring again to Him that sent me (1 Chronicles 21:9-12).

Here were David's options: three years of famine, three months of bloody warfare, or three days in the hand of the Lord. (You may also find an account of this story in Second Samuel 24.)

Even with options like these, David realized he would be better off in the hand of the Lord than anywhere else. David responded:

...I am in a great strait: let me fall now into the hand of the Lord; for very great are His mercies: but let me not fall into the hand of man (1 Chronicles 21:13).

David chose well. He knew three years with no rain was a long time. The crops would die, and so would thirsty humans. Three months of bloody warfare without God's favor was also more than David could bear. Three months in the hands of his enemies? No way! Imagine how horrible that would be!

That left only one option—to be dealt with for three short days, but nevertheless severely, by the hand of the Lord. David had confidence in God and recalled His many mercies. He remembered what it had been like to be in God's hand, reliant on His mercies. He chose God's hand because of His mercies.

The Attributes of Mercy

The mercy of God is like being in court, totally guilty of some crime—speeding, perhaps. The judge comes out and listens as you admit to him that you ran that stop sign, speeding. You're guilty. You know it. The judge knows it. The prosecuting attorney is crying out for your head on a plate: "Guilty! Guilty! 'Give him the chair'!" But mercy kicks in just then and you are released, acquitted. The mercy of God does not mean that you did nothing wrong; it means not getting the penalty you rightly deserve.

You did it. You knew you did it. You knew you deserved the full penalty of the law. Yet you got off... because God was merciful to you, a sinner.

That's how mercy operates.

Jesus is your ever-present Advocate, seated at the right hand of the Father making intercession for you. He's pleading your case, the best trial Lawyer there is. While the devil rails and demands you receive full sentence, Jesus is right there standing up for you and pleading for mercy.

Jesus is saying, "I know what the evidence is, and it doesn't look too good. But there was blood shed for that crime on Calvary, and it's covered. That sin, that crime, is covered." Hear the Judge, the Father, pronounce, "Mercy!"

David had confidence in the hand of the Lord and begged not to be given over into the hands of men.

You may put a lot of trust in your friends. Friends are good. But you can never fully trust people. You can appreciate them and the things that they may do. But people are people—human—and everyone has the capacity to let you down. They'll disappoint you: raise you up today and hang you tomorrow; pat you on the back in church and stab you in the back on the parking lot. David knew that. He chose to be personally dealt with by God rather than be given over into the untrustworthy hands of his enemies.

Although he didn't trust people, David did trust God. He may have forgotten God—just for a minute—but then he remembered His love, His grace, His goodness, His pity, His mercy...His hand.

In God's hand, there is longsuffering. There is power when you're weak. There is strength when you're down. There is prosperity. There's joy. There is peace in the midst of your troubles. In God's hand, there's a wife, a husband, brothers, sisters, and friends who will stick closer than a brother. But in the hand of man there is deceit, inconsistency, mistrust, betrayal, and unforgiveness. So David said, "Let me fall into God's hand."

So the Lord sent pestilence upon Israel: and there fell of Israel seventy thousand men. And God sent an angel unto Jerusalem to destroy it: and as he was destroying, the Lord beheld, and He repented Him of the evil, and said to the angel that destroyed, It is enough, stay now thine hand. And the angel of the Lord stood by the threshingfloor of Ornan the Jebusite (1 Chronicles 21:14-15).

And David began to be restored.

Look at Paul's understanding of the same concept.

Brethren, if a man be overtaken in a fault, ye which are spiritual, restore such an one in the spirit of meekness; considering thyself, lest thou also be tempted (Galatians 6:1).

God sent an angel to administer His justice because angels carry the Spirit of God, not the spirit of man. Angels are not like we are. They do not reproduce. They think like God. They encamp around us. They fight in the heavenlies. They undertake assignments from God on our behalf. When God sent pestilence in punishment of David's sin, it was sent through an angel. And 70,000 men died because of David's disobedience.

Even as the angel began to move through the land, God's heart was turned in compassion toward David and Israel. He may have thought about how much He loved David and their closeness of the past. He may have remembered calling David, "A man after My own heart" (1 Sam. 13:14; Acts 13:22). The Bible says God's heart was so moved that He "repented." God, who changes not, had a change of plans because He had a change of mind. He changed His plan and ordered the angel whose sword was already drawn to cease his destruction. God said, "It is enough!"

The angel stopped right in his tracks when God said, "STOP!"

And He's still doing it. By His hand of mercy upon our lives, God is saying, "STOP! Hold it! It is enough! I know he's guilty! I know he should get what he deserves, but I say, 'STOP!' "

That's why Jesus died—to pay the price for our sin so that God could put His hand over us and say to the devil, "STOP!"

And David lifted up his eyes, and saw the angel of the Lord stand between the earth and the heaven, having a drawn sword in his hand stretched out over Jerusalem. Then David and the elders of Israel, who were clothed in sackcloth, fell upon their faces. And David said unto God, Is it not I that commanded the people to be numbered? even I it is that have sinned and done evil indeed; but as for these sheep, what have they done? let Thine hand, I pray Thee, O Lord my God, be on me, and on my father's house; but not on Thy people, that they should be plagued. Then the angel of the Lord commanded Gad to say to David, that David should go up, and set up an altar unto the Lord in the threshingfloor of Ornan the Jebusite (1 Chronicles 21:16-18).

And God had mercy on David.

God's Bountiful Mercies

When God has mercy on you, something that was supposed to happen...doesn't. David knew about God's mercy. Otherwise he could not have written so powerfully of God's mercies in the Book of Psalms. Time after time, he had seen God's mercies. And now he had seen them again.

The hand of the Lord, full of mercy...something each one of us needs daily.

We depend on God's hand of mercy.

His mercy wakes us up each morning.

His mercy puts shelter over our heads.

His mercy walks with us.

His mercy puts food on our tables.

His mercy keeps the money coming in and the bills paid.

His mercy is there for us, morning, noon, and night!

It gives us peace.

It gives us joy.

It gives us grace.

Sweet, amazing, grace....

┌─────────┐
│   2   │
└─────────┘

God's Hand of Keeping Power

As we study the Word as it refers to the hand of the Lord, we discover that *the hand of the Lord* actually means "the power of God." Let me reintroduce you to the fact that we don't serve a weak God. We serve a powerful God! His power is not just any power. It's not natural power; it's supernatural—beyond the natural. *Super*-natural! He is an awesome God, and as believers in Christ, we must understand that we serve an awesome God. He is *all-powerful* in everything He does. He is a God who is everywhere; all-knowing, all-present, at all times. He's a mighty God. So there is no reason for those of us who are called of God to serve Him on the level of mediocrity, for we serve a God who is able to do exceedingly abundantly above all that we could ask or think (see Eph. 3:20).

No matter what it is that we are currently going through, that *all-powerful* God we serve is able to do exceedingly, abundantly above all that we could think or ask. He's able to cause all those circumstances coming against us right this minute to work for our good (see Rom. 8:28). He is able to produce power on our behalf to make each situation work out for our good. Now that's power!

Fear Not!

Yes, we serve a God of power and a God of promise—a supernatural God who gives us His Word that He will subdue our enemies and fight on our behalf. Yet so many of us continue to live in fear. God says, "Fear not!"

Fear thou not; for I am with thee: be not dismayed; for I am thy God: I will strengthen thee; yea, I will help thee; yea, I will uphold thee with the right hand of My righteousness. Behold, all they that were incensed against thee shall be ashamed and confounded: they shall be as nothing; and they that strive with thee shall perish (Isaiah 41:10-11).

In preparation to write this book I studied the many scriptural references to the hand of the Lord. I wanted to get a historical view of the text. When I got to chapter 41 of the Book of Isaiah, I began to realize that this text had application to our lives today reaching far beyond the simple historical application of what was happening in Israel at the time this passage was written.

I began to see the importance of our laying down our burdens of the past—those "yesterday" burdens we still carry into our "tomorrows." Those "yesterday" burdens can become hindrances that keep us from becoming what God intends us to become. As long as we continue to carry all that junk from the past, we can't go on with God.

There comes a point in life at which we must throw that junk down at the foot of the cross and trust, understanding that we serve a God who tells us to cast all our cares upon Him. (See 1 Peter 5:7.) That means we are to "Fear not..." just as stated in Isaiah 41:10. The meaning of that passage is simple; it means "Don't be afraid."

Many people today are living in fear. They have a spirit of fear. They're afraid of the dark; afraid to leave home; and afraid of what other people will think of them. That's bondage. You may think it is relying on common sense to be afraid of those kinds of things, but God didn't tell us to rely on common sense. He said, "Don't lean on your own understanding!" He said, "Acknowledge Me in all your ways!" (See Proverbs 3:5-6.)

So *fear not* means more than simply not being afraid. It also means, "Don't anticipate that something tragic is going to happen to you!" To live in fear is more than just being afraid all the time. It's also worrying about those things that haven't occurred yet. It's deciding in advance that the results of the medical test you will have next week will be positive and you'll be told you have that incurable disease you fear so much. It's anticipating that you won't be able to afford to pay for the college tuition of your son or daughter before they've even enrolled in college (and high-school graduation is still twelve months away)! It's anticipating you won't be able to meet your budget for this year, and last year isn't over yet! It's anticipating you'll fail before you've even taken the test, anticipating you won't make it when you've just begun your journey.

Fear is forecasting tragedy, then sitting back and waiting for it to happen. But the Word of God says, "Fear not!" *Anticipate not!* There are many things that are bound to happen whether or you fear them or not; death, for instance. You may be afraid of dying, but whether you fear it or not, one day you will still die. Death is inevitable. Why fear something you have no power to keep from happening? When it's your time to go, you'll go. That's it—no negotiating. You will leave planet Earth at the exact moment that it is your time to die. But that's okay, because to be absent from the body is to be present with the Lord (see 2 Cor. 5:8). Why anticipate death? Why not instead anticipate being present with the Lord? *Fear not!*

Many of the things we anticipate, we speak. Then they come to pass. For instance, I have had a tendency to become sleepy when I drive. I'd start thinking about those 1,200 miles I had left to drive and get sleepy just thinking about it. I would just anticipate becoming sleepy, and then I'd reach over and tap my wife, Pam, on the shoulder. "Honey, I think I'm getting sleepy; you drive!" And she'd switch places with me and drive, even though we were just 30 minutes out! Now, it doesn't look very manly to be knocked out, the kids knocked out in the back seat, while your sweet little wife does all the driving! It's better to not look manly than to drive deadly, granted; but I got the victory over that sleepy demon because I trained myself to stop anticipating getting sleepy behind the wheel. I stopped speaking about how sleepy I was. Instead, I declared I was going to have a great day and drive all the way to our destination. What I anticipated began to come to pass; I could drive the entire way without becoming too sleepy to safely stay behind the wheel. This is just an example of how we can change those things we anticipate, and therefore change the results in our lives.

Why We Shouldn't Fear

God gives us good reasons to fear not. The first good reason is because His presence is with us. In Isaiah 41:10, He tells us, "Fear not...." Why? "For I am with thee." We have the assurance of the presence of God with us. Therefore, *fear not!*

When everything is dark all around you and you can't see what's ahead, *fear not!* Even though you cannot see the physical presence of God, you have His Word that He is with you, and in faith you can believe that even in the dark of night, He is there. During your greatest time of burden, in the midst of the greatest trial, He is there with you. He says, "Lo, I am with you alway, even unto the end of the world..." (Mt. 28:20). That means He is with you all the way through eternity! Just think about that: to the end of time! No matter where you go, what you do, He'll be there with you. In the midst of your troubles, in the midst of your trials, God is there.

There is no place you can go to be absent from God because He is everywhere, always present, never moving. Even though there will be trouble—and the Word of God assures there will be trouble—He is there. When you stand before your "Goliath" and people are laughing at how small and weak you are, He is there to help you face that giant. You can safely tell your Goliath, "Before you start laughing, I want you to know that I brought somebody with me, and greater is He that is in me than he that is in the world!" (See 1 John 4:4b.)

There is never a time when you should count God absent. In the heat of the battle, He is there—ever present, never absent. He has a perfect attendance record. In fact, He is there for you right now.

God is the fourth man in the flames with you, just as He was present with Shadrach, Meschach, and Abednego in the fiery furnace. He's not like some of your friends who say, "Listen, man—I'll talk with you later!" when the heat's turned up. No, God is saying, "Trust Me! You're going to make it, and everything's going to be all right! Come on, stand behind Me! You're going to make it through this thing!" That's the God we serve!

We have God's presence with us, and for that reason, He says, "Fear not!" We also have a personal relationship with Him, and that's another good reason to live above fear.

Let's look at Isaiah 41:10 again: "Fear thou not; for I am with thee: be not dismayed; for I am thy God...." That's a personal relationship! "I'm your God! Don't be afraid!" One of the biggest reasons we feel defeated in the midst of trials and tribulations is that we really don't know God personally. We know just what we hear others say about Him. That's not personal. That's not relational. That's *informational.*

But I'm talking about relationship. To be in a relationship with someone means to be close to them, to see the way they operate, to observe them and hear the way they talk. It means to become involved with that person and get to know them. It means to communicate with them, hold their hand, walk with them, talk with them. You can't do that from a distance. You have to draw near a person in order to get to know them intimately. It's the only way you'll get to know another person. It's the same with God.

You can't get to know God from a distance. You have to draw near and develop a relationship with Him. You do that through prayer. You can get information about Him at church services. But to get to know Him, you have to get alone with Him in your prayer closet. Those are the times when you'll say to Him, "Now, God, I read 'fear not' in the Bible, and I need to know more about what that means. I'm in a jam right now and it looks like there's no way out. You tell me not to fear. You tell me You'll make a way where there is no way and help me. You tell me, according to Your Word, that You are bread in a starving land. I don't know how I'm going to pay my bills and feed my children. I don't know how I'm going to meet my business obligations. But I want to get to know You. I'm going to talk with You, and I know You'll help me."

That's how you get to know Him. That's how you develop a personal relationship with Him, a relationship based on love and trust. You've got to learn to know Him more than simply through the eyes of Isaiah, Abraham, Isaac, or Jacob. You've got to know Him for yourself, not merely through the eyes of Matthew, Mark, Luke, and John. You've got to know Him for yourself, not only through the eyes of Peter and Paul. And as you do, He will say, "I am *your* God! Not just Isaiah's God, not just Abraham's God, not just Paul's God—I am *your God!*"

As you develop such a relationship with God, an intimate relationship, you will hear Him speak to your heart and your ear. He will whisper sweet things in your ear. He'll tell you how much He loves you, how special you are to Him, how much victory you have in Him, how much good health, how much provision—all because of your relationship with Him.

You can't have victory in your Christian walk while trying to know God from a distance. You must know Him personally. When when you do, it won't matter what the devil is telling you because you'll know the truth: He's *your God.*

When your credit's turned down, when you didn't get that job you deserved, when you're kicked to the side of the road by life's circumstances, you'll still be able to sense God's presence and hear Him say, "You are My friend, just as Abraham was My friend!" He wants to be in relationship with you so that you will never again doubt His existence. He is there for you—personally.

A third reason not to fear is that His power is available to us. Isaiah 41:10 says, "...I will strengthen thee; yea, I will help thee; yea, I will uphold thee with the right hand of My righteousness." Not only will He strengthen you, but He will uphold you with the right hand of His *righteousness*, which means "transferred holiness."

Because God is a righteous God, nothing short of righteousness will please Him. The Word of God says that without holiness, no man shall see God (see Heb. 12:14). But because you and I are messed up creatures, we have no chance at holiness except through Him. In and of ourselves we don't have what it takes to approach God. We ought not to even be in His presence. But when God transfers His holiness to us—His righteousness—although He can't come down to our level, we can come up to His level. We can qualify to be in His presence through His righteousness that has been transferred to us. We're too carnal to get it on our own; but when God gives it to us, we can come up to where He is, on His throne of righteousness, and speak to Him as His friend.

Because of what Jesus did upon the cross at Calvary, we are able to approach God as righteous. Because Jesus died for our sins, we have been given some of His righteousness, some of His holiness, so that we might be declared righteous and holy before God. He says, "I will uphold you. I will strengthen you. I will give you My strength. I will give you My righteousness so that when I get ready to do what I'm going to do, you will look like I want you to look. What I will see when I look at you will be an image of Me. I'll see a part of Me in you so that when I look at you, I will see Me. When I bless you, I bless Me. When I take care of you, I take care of Me."

That's what it's all about!

Let's look at Isaiah 41:11-13 in the New American Standard version:

Behold, all those who are angered at you will be shamed and dishonored; those who contend with you will be as nothing, and will perish. You will seek those who quarrel with you, but will not find them. Those who war with you will be as nothing, and non-existent. For I am the Lord your God, who upholds your right hand, who says to you, "Do not fear, I will help you."

What fantastic promises, and all because He is our God—all-powerful—in loving, personal relationship with us! Why fear? He is for us! What supernatural power!

God, Our Keeper

He promises to keep us safe, to walk with us, to talk with us, to surround us with Himself. He promises to protect us, to cause our circumstances to work out in a way that will bless us. He promises these things, and He tells us not to fear.

God is our Keeper, and His keeping power is available to us. When the hand of the Lord is upon our lives, it is sometimes for the purpose of keeping us in the midst of troubles. Sometimes it keeps us from trouble.

Sometimes it protects us from our enemies. But each time, we have the assurance that God is there for us and that His hand is upon our lives.

3

God's Hand of Blessing

All blessings are in the hand of God—that pay raise, that new house, that new car, every blessing! All are blessings from the hand of God. I'm not talking about good luck; I'm talking about blessings. Your blessings are in the hand of God.

Are you in line for the blessings of God?

The first question I must ask is: *Are you saved?* Are you sure? Are you saved *and* sure? I'm not asking whether you're a member of some church. I'm asking whether you're saved. Have you been regenerated? Reborn? Have you been transformed by the renewing of your mind? Have you met Jesus Christ as your personal Savior, and have you invited Him into your life? Have you accepted Him? Many people invite Him in, then don't accept Him. They reject Him when they discover that to serve Him means to change the way they've been living.

The next question I must ask is, *Do you love God?* Do you reverence Him? I'm not talking about a feeling; I'm talking about that which moves you to honor and obey Him. Do you really love God?

The third question is, *Do you believe that the Word of God is really the whole truth and nothing but the truth?* Do you believe the Word of God—inside and out, front to back, Old Testament through New Testament—is the Truth?

Next, *Do you trust Him?* I'm not talking about trusting God to do what you want Him to do; I'm talking about trusting God in the unseen, when you can't see what lies ahead. Do you trust God unequivocally?

Are you serious about your walk with Christ? Or is it just a Sunday-morning thing with you? If it's just a church thing, a going-through-the-motions kind of thing, then you're not serious. But if you *are* serious, then I have another question for you.

Do you want to be blessed?

To Be Blessed by God...

Do you want to be blessed, or are you satisfied with the status quo, the way things are? Can you handle being blessed? I'm not talking about getting some goodie now and then from Santa Claus or the tooth fairy. No—I'm talking about God blessing you. Can you stand for God to bless you? Or would you just turn into a nut and stop praying, stop worshiping, stop praising Him? You know, some people can't stand it when God begins to bless them. They sit down on the job and lose their ground with Him.

But let me tell you something: We are the ones who control the blessings of God. Every blessing, we control. That's right! The blessings of God are in His hand, but we control them.

Would you, as a parent, withhold blessings from your children? No, you'd give your children whatever they wanted—even if they knowingly, willingly were walking in disobedience. You would keep on giving to them, keep on blessing them, because you love them. You may sit them down and give them step-by-step instructions from time to time, but even when they disobey those instructions, you would keep right on blessing them and providing for their needs. But when it became apparent to you that your children were in total disobedience—not just occasional disobedience—what then? Would you keep on blessing them in spite of that total disobedience? Or would you draw the line once it became obvious that they knew the rules and yet decided to break them in defiance of the consequences?

Think about it....

The Release of God's Blessings

As we continue in our study of the hand of God, we will learn how to release a continual outpouring of the blessings of God. My understanding of the definition of being blessed by God is to be in a position or posture of having all one's needs met as they occur. You may say, "Well, preacher, that's not very realistic." Maybe not, according to man. But it's very realistic, according to God;

because He has promised that He will supply all our needs (see Phil. 4:19). He also promises that if we seek Him and His righteousness first, then all things will be added unto us (see Mt. 6:33). That means you and me.

But there is a priority that we must set in order to receive the release of God's blessings. Many people say, "If God blesses me, then I'll set things right." No, that's not the way it goes. It doesn't work like that. It's not get riches, then get righteous. It's get righteous, then get riches. You can have the riches of God, but first you must have the righteousness of God. The blessings of God are in His hand to be released to us when we are obedient to Him. If we don't obey Him, He won't bless us. As we learn to obey Him, He will bless us. When we submit ourselves to the authority of God, He will bless us.

The reason we're being blessed by Him is that we are committed to the Word of God. But if tomorrow we were to decide to return to Egypt, the blessings would cease. So we decide how it will be, blessed or not blessed. We make the determination.

You may be in a day-to-day struggle just to walk with Him. It may be a daily battle. You're striving hard to walk with Him—praying, fasting, working at it. But it just keeps getting tougher and tougher. That's why you keep on going to church. You're not there to dress up and see people; you're there to learn about the Word of God. You don't care whether you cry off all your makeup in public or whether your mascara runs. You're there to praise Him and magnify His name!

You're there because of your obedience. You're in church because you are making yourself available to God. You're being obedient, and even when people are challenging you, even when they're saying you're crazy, even when others are trying to get you to turn away from God, you're hanging in there with Him. You're refusing to go back to Egypt because of your obedience to the Word of God. You're not questioning what God is saying; you're trusting Him. You're taking Him at His Word, by faith. That's why the blessings of God are being released to you.

Let's look at Malachi, chapter 3:

For I am the Lord, I change not; therefore ye sons of Jacob are not consumed. Even from the days of your fathers ye are gone away from Mine ordinances, and have not kept them. Return unto Me, and I will return unto you, saith the Lord of hosts. But ye said, Wherein shall we return? Will a man rob God? Yet ye have robbed Me. But ye say, Wherein have we robbed Thee? In tithes and offerings. Ye are cursed with a curse: for ye have robbed Me, even this whole nation. Bring ye all the tithes into the storehouse, that there may be meat in Mine house, and prove Me now herewith, saith the Lord of hosts, if I will not open you the windows of heaven, and pour you out a blessing, that there shall not be room enough to receive it. And I will rebuke the devourer for your sakes, and he shall not destroy the fruits of your ground; neither shall your vine cast her fruit before the time in the field, saith the Lord of hosts. And all nations shall call you blessed: for ye shall be a delightsome land, saith the Lord of hosts (Malachi 3:6-12).

Malachi, the last book of the Old Testament, was written at the beginning of the 400-year period of silence during which Israel did not hear substantially from God. Not until the events recorded in the Book of Matthew, which occurred about 400 years later, did the Lord again begin to speak to His people. Malachi 3:6 says, "For I am the Lord; I change not...." People may change. Circumstances may change. But God does not change. He is the same today, yesterday, and tomorrow (Heb. 13:8). What He said 400 years ago is still the truth today. What He said 2,000 years ago still remains true. He is the same today and throughout infinity. No matter how we may try to dissect it theologically, no matter how we may try to interpret it intellectually, God's Word is true now and for all time.

People are not that way. Today, they're there for you. Tomorrow, they're gone. They may promise to be there for you always, but one minute you see them, the next you don't. People are just not reliable. One day you may be able to rely on them, but the next, they may let you down. God is not like that. He is totally, 100 percent reliable 100 percent of the time. He changes not. He's the same always—today, yesterday, tomorrow, forever. He says, in this passage, "Return unto Me...I will return unto you..." (Mal. 3:7b). You can count on that because God said it. Notice, however, that He didn't just say, "I'm going to come unto you." He said, "Return unto Me and [then] I will return unto you." In other words, "You show up, and I'll show up. You be obedient unto Me, and I'll come through for you."

Yet many of us continue to pray for God to bless us while we do nothing to merit those blessings. We just holler, "God bless me! God give me this! God give me that!" God says, "Well, come on up here where I am and get it! I'm not coming down to your level. You come up to Mine. I know your heart. I can see right past all those hallelujahs! I can see beyond your praises; I can see beyond tongues. I know your heart! That's what I'm watching! When your heart changes, I'll change. You can't move Me by the words of your mouth, by naming it, claiming it, and framing it. That doesn't mean a thing, if you're not changing. If you're not coming up to where I am, if you're not being obedient, I will not return unto you. But if you return unto Me, I will return unto you. And then I will bless you!"

There is no negotiating with the Lord Most High! We don't control Him, but we do control whether or not He blesses us by our obedience to Him. We don't dictate to Him; He dictates to us. It's up to us to come up to His standards. Because of Jesus' finished work upon the cross, we can do that. When we're sick, He won't come down to us. We must come up to where He is—where healing is. When we're in need, He won't come down to us; we've got to come up to where He is—where provision is.

God is not some cosmic bellhop. We don't ring for Him and watch Him come running. No, Church, it's time to snap out of it and get our act together. It's time for us to return to Him. Then He will return to us and bless us—abundantly, supernaturally, above all we can ask or think, above all we can comprehend!

Do you want to be blessed? Do you really want to be blessed? Then understand that God has a record of everything you say and do. He knows about the cheating. He knows all about the game-playing. He knows about the ways you've been tripping on Him; He knows each one of your thoughts. He knows all about *you*! You can't get anything over on God. You're made in His image, and He didn't make you to play games!

So, do you want to be blessed? Then return to Him. Stop robbing Him. And by that, I don't mean ripping off the church or some preacher. I mean what it says in the Word of God. Stop stealing from God by withholding tithes and offerings. When you made a hundred dollars and decided to give God only a dollar of it back, you robbed Him. If you didn't give God a tenth of your income, you robbed Him. You can't be blessed while you're robbing God.

A man in our congregation tells the story of how he and his sister watched his mama put money into a jar on a shelf in the pantry. They'd go in there sometimes and sneak money out of it. So when Easter came around that year, they had no new clothes to wear to church on Easter Sunday. Everybody else got new clothes, but not those two. Their mama knew what they had done and confronted them: "Every time you went into that jar, you took a little of what your daddy and I had put aside for your new Easter outfits. You robbed your own benefactor. Your blessings were in that jar, and you stole your own blessings."

That's a good example of what this passage in Malachi means. By robbing God, you're robbing your own Benefactor.

Sure, there are bills due. That's why you need to make sure you pay God His ten percent. Ministries have work they need to do to benefit their communities, but they can't do the work at hand because the storehouse isn't full. The storehouse isn't full because the people are not tithing and giving offerings. Twenty percent of the church, by estimate, supports 100 percent of the work, and 100 percent of the people benefit. Think what could be done if everyone chose obedience to God's Word according to Malachi, chapter 3!

How to Receive God's Blessings

Do you want to be blessed? Malachi, chapter 3, says you are cursed with a curse if you rob God. How can you be blessed and cursed at the same time? God says we are to bring the tithes and offerings into the storehouse, then see if there will not be a blessing so large that there's not even room to receive it. The storehouse is the church, the place where people come for refuge, for redemption, for restoration. They come for shelter from the storms of life, for teaching, and to learn how to reach a lost and dying world with the message of Jesus Christ.

When we start putting our resources into the storehouse, as God commands, He will open the windows of heaven and pour blessings out upon us. This is no savings and loan; this is the Church, and we are the Body of Christ. Talk about saving for a rainy day! When we invest in God's business, He will invest in ours! It's up to us to take care of the poor. When we do that, God will bless us. When we do that, God will rebuke the devourer. When we do that, God will give back to us abundantly even more than we gave to Him.

Think about it: This nation of ours is one place on Earth that should not be broke. We should not be in debt. It is a misrepresentation of the character of God when His Church is in bondage to debt. It is a misrepresentation of the character of God when there are hungry people to be fed and when there is ministry to be done but not enough money to do it with. It's a misrepresentation of God to scheme and stretch and shuffle and hustle in order to make things happen for the Church. We should have more than enough coming in with which to do the work of God.

We Are Abraham's Seed

God made Abraham some promises long ago, and those promises are for you and I today. I know, I know—we're not Jewish; how can those promises be for you and I today? Because we are *the seed of Abraham, by faith*. We have been adopted into His lineage. Let's study Romans, chapter 4, for a better understanding of what I mean:

Therefore it is of faith, that it might be by grace; to the end the promise might be sure to all the seed; not to that only which is of the law, but to that also which is of the faith of Abraham; who is the father of us all, (As it is written, I have made thee a father of many nations,) before Him whom he believed, even God, who quickeneth the dead, and calleth those things which be not as though they were. Who against hope believed in hope, that he might become the father of many nations, according to that which was spoken, So shall thy seed be. And being not weak in faith, he considered not his own body now dead, when he was about an hundred years old, neither yet the deadness of Sarah's womb: He staggered not at the promise of God through unbelief; but was strong in faith, giving glory to God; and being fully persuaded that, what He had promised, He was able also to perform (Romans 4:16-21).

In this passage of text, God is reminding the Church that Abraham believed Him even when circumstances dictated otherwise. He and his wife were both old, yet they continued to believe God for the child through which Abraham would become father to many nations. God was saying to an aged Abraham, "I'm going to resurrect you; I'm going to resurrect your sexuality. I'm going to resurrect the deadness in you and in Sarah, and she will have a child." Based on those promises, Abraham hoped and believed. He believed everything God had promised him. But time passed, and still there was no child.

So Sarah sent for Hagar....

Romans 4:20 says Abraham "...staggered not at the promise of God through unbelief...." Sarah, however, was another matter. She sent for her Egyptian servant, Hagar, and ordered her to sleep with Abraham. The child she conceived was *not* the child of promise God had spoken of, but he was a child conceived and born as a work of the flesh.

Yet Abraham continued to believe God's promise to him—by faith. And, by faith, Sarah conceived in old age, and Isaac, the child of promise, was born to Abraham.

We are Abraham's seed by faith. Thus, every promise God made to Abraham is ours—by faith. Because we are believers in Jesus Christ, we are Abraham's seed. Like Israel, we are a blessed people, but we are also a disobedient people. Like Israel, we are hardheaded. And until we learn to trust God enough to release the ten percent tithe that is rightfully His, we are limiting the ministry of Jesus Christ on Earth. We should not be relying on the world's system for our supply; the world's system should be relying on us.

The Blessing of God's Healing

...If thou wilt diligently hearken to the voice of the Lord thy God, and wilt do that which is right in His sight, and wilt give ear to His commandments, and keep all His statutes, I will put none of these diseases upon thee, which I have brought upon the Egyptians: for I am the Lord that healeth thee (Exodus 15:26).

Healing is part of God's blessing. Do you think it is a hard thing for God to heal someone? Do you think it's complicated to be healed by God? It isn't if you're blessed by Him. We've already talked about the tithe and how in tithing we are removing the curse and coming under the blessings of God. Once we are obedient to Him with our tithes and offerings, we're in line to be blessed by Him. Thus, when sickness and curses come upon others, those things won't come near your household. That's what the Word says!

God takes care of His own! In fact, the Word says:

Now therefore, if ye will obey My voice indeed, and keep My covenant, then ye shall be a peculiar treasure unto Me above all people: for all the earth is Mine: And ye shall be unto Me a kingdom of priests, and an holy nation. These are the words which thou shalt speak unto the children of Israel (Exodus 19:5-6).

In these verses, the Lord is saying, "Even though all nations are Mine, I'll make something special out of you!" He says, "I want to make you extra-special! Just do what I say—that's all it takes. It's that simple!"

Now, let's look at Exodus 23:20-26 in the New International Version:

See, I am sending an angel ahead of you to guard you along the way and to bring you to the place I have prepared. Pay attention to him and listen to what he says. Do not rebel against him; he will not forgive your rebellion, since My Name is in him. If you listen carefully to what he says and do all that I say, I will be an enemy to your enemies and will oppose those who oppose you. My angel will go ahead of you and bring you into the land of the Amorites, Hittites, Perizzites, Canaanites, Hivites and Jebusites, and I will wipe them out. Do not bow down before their gods or worship them or follow their practices. You must demolish them and break their sacred stones to pieces. Worship the Lord your God, and His blessing will be on your food and water. I will take away sickness from among you, and none will miscarry or be barren in your land. I will give you a full life span.

God's Promises of Blessing From Scripture

Do you want to be blessed? In the Scriptures the Lord promises again and again to bless His people.

If ye walk in My statutes, and keep My commandments, and do them; then I will give you rain in due season, and the land shall yield her increase, and the trees of the field shall yield their fruit. And your threshing shall reach unto the vintage, and the vintage shall reach unto the sowing time: and ye shall eat your bread to the full, and dwell in your land safely. And I will give peace in the land, and ye shall lie down, and none shall make you afraid: and I will rid evil beasts out of the land, neither shall the sword go through your land. And ye shall chase your enemies, and they shall fall before you by the sword. And five of you shall chase an hundred, and an hundred of you shall put ten thousand to flight: and your enemies shall fall before you by the sword. For I will have respect unto you, and make you fruitful, and multiply you, and establish My covenant with you. And ye shall eat old store, and bring forth the old because of the new. And I will set My tabernacle among you: and My soul shall not abhor you. And I will walk among you, and will be your God, and ye shall be My people. I am the Lord your God, which brought you forth out of the land of Egypt, that ye should not be their bondmen; and

I have broken the bands of your yoke, and made you go upright (Leviticus 26:3-13).

Sounds like blessings to me! But don't stop; keep going to Deuteronomy 4:40:

Thou shalt keep therefore His statutes, and His commandments, which I command thee this day, that it may go well with thee, and with thy children after thee, and that thou mayest prolong thy days upon the earth, which the Lord thy God giveth thee, for ever.

Does that sound like a blessing? Yes! But don't stop there, either. Keep going to Deuteronomy 5:29:

O that there were such an heart in them, that they would fear Me, and keep all My commandments always, that it might be well with them, and with their children for ever!

It sounds like God wants to bless His children, not only in this generation, but in the generations to come! By our obedience, we can build a foundation of faith and blessings for our children and our children's children!

Now these are the commandments, the statutes, and the judgments, which the Lord your God commanded to teach you, that ye might do them in the land whither ye go to possess it (Deuteronomy 6:1).

Behold, I set before you this day a blessing and a curse; a blessing, if ye obey the commandments of the Lord your God, which I command you this day: and a curse, if ye will not obey the commandments of the Lord your God, but turn aside out of the way which I command you this day, to go after other gods, which ye have not known (Deuteronomy 11:26-28).

Do you see? God wants to bless us, but He can only do so as a result of our obedience to His Word and the statutes and commands set forth in it. We have the ability to choose—blessings or curses.

Observe and hear all these words which I command thee, that it may go well with thee, and with thy children after thee for ever, when thou doest that which is good and right in the sight of the Lord thy God (Deuteronomy 12:28).

...Save when there shall be no poor among you; for the Lord shall greatly bless thee in the land which the Lord thy God giveth thee for an inheritance to possess it: Only if thou carefully hearken unto the voice of the Lord thy God, to observe to do all these commandments which I command thee this day. For the Lord thy God blesseth thee, as He promised thee: and thou shalt lend unto many nations, but thou shalt not borrow; and thou shalt reign over many nations, but they shall not reign over thee. If there be among you a poor man of one of thy brethren within any of thy gates in thy land which the Lord thy God giveth thee, thou shalt not harden thine heart, nor shut thine hand from thy poor brother: But thou shalt open thine hand wide unto him, and shalt surely lend him sufficient for his need, in that which he wanteth. Beware that there be not a thought in thy wicked heart, saying, The seventh year, the year of release, is at hand; and thine eye be evil against thy poor brother, and thou givest him nought; and he cry unto

the Lord against thee, and it be sin unto thee (Deuter-onomy 15:4-9).

Stop right there! The Word is saying, "Lend freely and don't even think about the debt being paid back." That's not why you're giving; you're giving to be a bless-ing, and you will receive blessing from the hand of the Lord.

Now, let's go on:

Thou shalt surely give him, and thine heart shall not be grieved when thou givest unto him: because that for this thing the Lord thy God shall bless thee in all thy works, and in all that thou puttest thine hand unto. For the poor shall never cease out of the land: therefore I com-mand thee, saying, Thou shalt open thine hand wide unto thy brother, to thy poor, and to thy needy, in thy land (Deuteronomy 15:10-11).

There is great blessing in giving freely to our brothers and sisters in need! But blessing comes only when we give without grumbling and complaint. Remember, we are the ones who shall lend and not borrow (see Deut. 28:12); we are God's children, and His blessings are upon us.

Keep therefore the words of this covenant, and do them, that ye may prosper in all that ye do (Deuteronomy 29:9).

See, I have set before thee this day life and good, and death and evil; In that I command thee this day to love the Lord thy God, to walk in His ways, and to keep His commandments and His statutes and His judgments, that thou mayest live and multiply: and the Lord thy

God shall bless thee in the land whither thou goest to possess it (Deuteronomy 30:15-16).

Keep on serving Him; keep on walking in obedience to Him; keep on choosing good and doing good, and you have His Word: God will bless you! When you begin to give according to His Word, He will not just bless you; He will multiply you! That's what He did when He blessed the loaves and fishes—He multiplied them. Those meager provisions fed thousands, with some left over. That's what He will do for you.

The Blessing of Peace

Finally, He will bless you with peace, and not just any kind of peace. He will bless you by providing peace with your enemies. Proverbs 16:7 says, "When a man's ways please the Lord, He maketh even his enemies to be at peace with him." That's what He will do for you. And what a blessing it is to be at peace with your enemies! When you are walking in a way that is pleasing to God, He will move heaven and earth on your behalf to make you at peace with your enemies. He will make them wind up liking you! He will make them your footstool (Ps. 110:1). He will bring them over to your side.

These are just some of the ways God will bless you once you understand His hand of blessing and how to activate it in your life. Let me say it again: You don't control God; He controls you. But you do control the blessings of God. You can release them into your life, or you can cause them to be withheld.

It is your choice. Choose you this day....

4

God's Hand of Deliverance

Wherefore say unto the children of Israel, I am the Lord, and I will bring you out from under the burdens of the Egyptians, and I will rid you out of their bondage, and I will redeem you with a stretched out arm, and with great judgments: And I will take you to Me for a people, and I will be to you a God: and ye shall know that I am the Lord your God, which bringeth you out from under the burdens of the Egyptians. And I will bring you in unto the land, concerning the which I did swear to give it to Abraham, to Isaac, and to Jacob; and I will give it you for an heritage: I am the Lord (Exodus 6:6-8).

Throughout the Bible, we hear of many mighty, miraculous deliverances performed by God. There are the incredible deliverances from the hand of the enemy, such as the Lord's parting of the Red Sea to allow the Israelites safe passage from the Egyptians. There are deliverances from disease, like on Passover when the blood on the lintels of the doors kept the Israelites safe during the siege of the death angel. There are deliverances from hard labor, like when the Lord ended Jacob's service to Laban after many years of hard labor to earn the hand of Rachel. There are also deliverances from spiritual oppression, as when Jesus cast the demons from the Gadarene demoniac.

Many of us are in need of deliverance today, whether it be from the hand of the enemy, from circumstances and situations beyond our control that have us bound, or from actual spiritual oppression when unseen forces attempt to hold us captive.

But to understand how God's hand of deliverance operates in the life of a believer, we must first understand the Source of our deliverance.

The Lord, Our Source

To interpret correctly what it means to be delivered, I want to focus on the Deliverer. Who is our Deliverer? The Lord is our Deliverer! He is the Source! We may often find ourselves in circumstances in the natural that are so binding—situations that have us so painted into the corner—that it will take nothing short of God's supernatural power to get us out.

So let's refer to this passage in the Book of Exodus for a parallel between the circumstances surrounding the children of Israel and those things we face on Earth today:

Wherefore say unto the children of Israel, I am the Lord, and I will bring you out from under the burdens of the

Egyptians, and I will rid you out of their bondage, and I will redeem you with a stretched out arm, and with great judgments (Exodus 6:6).

These people were in an unusual situation: They were in bondage. But God promised to bring them out of that bondage—"with a stretched out arm"—by His hand of deliverance. The Lord said through His servant Moses, "I am the Lord, and I will bring you out...." It was never the intention of God for His people to be under the control of anyone but Him.

Are you under the control of circumstances today that are contrary to God's will for your life? Are you under the control of problems? What do you say when people ask you how you're doing? Do you respond, "I'm okay—*under the circumstances*"? That's not God's plan for you. He intends to lift you above those circumstances so that you may have victory over them. He said to the Israelites, just as He says to you today, "I am the Lord, and I will bring you out...."

When you wonder how you're going to work things out; when you ask yourself over and over, *What am I going to do?* When you wonder, *How can I do this thing?* Stop! Don't take a tranquilizer. Don't reach for a drink. Settle down and get before God. Then ask Him, "Lord, bring me out, just as You promised the Israelites!"

He is your Source—the Source of your deliverance from circumstances that have you hedged in. There are times when we are all placed in situations that are beyond our control. These can include the economy and the way the world's system is structured, with all the unfair things that go along with it—racial prejudices, economic boundaries. We didn't ask for that stuff. These things were born out of man's desire to be in control, to be smarter than he actually is. And sometimes that puts us in a bind.

But God reminds us that regardless of our circumstances, regardless of what man does to us, He will bring us up. He says to His children, "I am going to get you up and out from under everything that is oppressing you." You may sit there in church on Sunday morning and look like you have it all together, but come on, tell the truth! How about that unsaved husband waiting at home for you? It's just hell for you to go home—tell the truth! There's a fight waiting to happen when you go home. Or how about those rebellious children who won't have anything to do with church? What about them? Tell the truth—they're oppressing you and you just don't know what to do! Or how about that boss who has singled you out to pick on day after day because he's an unbeliever and he knows you're sold out to Jesus Christ? Tell the truth! Or how about your bank account? Tell the truth— you can't write checks because they're bouncing faster than you can get money into your account. Jesus knows! He's the Answer! He's the One who promises to get you out from under these and other circumstances and put you over to victory!

I hear people say all the time, "As soon as I get it together...." And to them, I say, "Forget it! You'll never get it together. You don't have what it takes to get it together.

If you had sense enough to fix it all along, how did it get into the shape it's in?" Admit it! You're messed up because you don't know what you're doing. You don't know everything, after all. Your IQ may be high on paper, but the truth is you're getting kicked around the block an awful lot for someone who's as smart as you. The devil is having a field day with you, but God says, "Don't worry! I am the Lord, and I will bring you out...."

There are times each one of us gets into messes beyond our control. Then we must look to God to get us out. By His hand of deliverance, we are set free from these insurmountable circumstances. He is the Source of our deliverance.

His Grace Is Sufficient

We all mess up. We buy $500 suits when the budget will only allow us to spend ninety-nine bucks. We buy a Mercedes Benz when there is only enough left each month to pay for a Hyundai. We're in debt to the hilt because we got ourselves there. But God says, "My grace is sufficient; *I am the Lord, and I will bring you out!*"

Hallelujah! You know you messed up. I know I messed up. We messed up. And God says, "I know all about it; *I am the Lord, and I will bring you out!* You got yourself into that mess. But I will extend mercy to you because I am the Source of your deliverance!"

You may be in your current situation because you have not yet learned to give God the glory. The Lord will go to extremes to make you take your own individual

"Isaacs" up to the mountaintop and sacrifice them there. He wants the glory!

If ever a place on Earth was in need of deliverance, it's the United States of America. And it will take more than a Constitution to make it happen. It will require the sovereign power of an Almighty God. God is bringing this nation to a point where there is no place left to go but down. There are men and women all across the United States who are so impressed with themselves that they're taking all the credit for their accomplishments—credit that is rightfully due the Lord. He's saying, "Okay, since you're up there so high, let's see what you'll do when you need My help." But listen: God allows us, even as a nation, to get into circumstances now and then where there is no place to turn but to Him. He wants the glory! The Word says, "I will lift up mine eyes unto the hills, from whence cometh my help. My help cometh from the Lord, which made heaven and earth" (Ps. 121:1-2). We may look everywhere for answers, but the Lord is our Help.

Consider the case of Nineveh, an evil city that God had every intention of wiping off the face of the earth. Yet because He is merciful, He sent Jonah to Nineveh to warn the city's inhabitants of their need to repent and turn from their evil, or they would receive the consequences of the Lord's wrath.

Jonah did not want to go to Nineveh. He resisted the Lord's command and wound up at the bottom of the sea inside the belly of a fish. God will do the same today:

He'll put you in the midst of a situation so big, there's no understanding it. And after He has taught you what it is you need to learn there, He will move the hand of His deliverance and get you out. Immediately! In the meantime, He'll have you there, inside the belly of the fish, praying for not just one hour but hours upon end each day. He'll have you studying the Word. He'll have you on your face, crying out to Him. While all hell is breaking loose around you, God will have you right where He wants you—in position to receive from His hand of deliverance when the right moment comes. Until then, you might as well stay put. What are you going to do? Buy your way out? You can't do that. You have to stay there, crying, "Father, I stretch my hands out to Thee! You are my Source of deliverance!" I don't care who you are or what family you came from. Regardless of your background or your position in life, you won't get true deliverance until God gives it to you. The devil may sometimes fool you into thinking you have real deliverance, but you're just out on probation—temporarily! The devil may have temporarily bailed you out, but you're still in bondage; and you will remain there until Jesus sets you free. Jesus is the only answer! "If the Son therefore shall make you free, ye shall be free indeed" (Jn. 8:36).

God's Sovereign Power

Have you ever stopped to think about the fact that every breath you take is a reminder of the sovereignty of God? In Him you *live* and *move* and have your *being* (see Acts 17:28). He is the reason you breathe; and when your time is up on Earth, you'll cease to breathe. And if you're a believer, you'll immediately enter His presence. Even if you do not know the Lord and have not accepted Him as Savior, every breath you breathe is due to Him. When it's time for you to leave this earth, you will still depart—right on schedule. Only you will not spend eternity with Him; instead, you will spend eternity in the place the Bible calls hell. Either way, the air you breathe is due to the sovereignty of God and the fact that it is His will that you continue to breathe and live and move and have your being.

You may exercise, you may eat right, you may stay in shape; yet these things mean nothing in God's scheme of things. He can take you at any minute. In fact, overreliance on good health can be a kind of bondage. You need to be spiritually free and realize that paying attention to your health is good—but no matter how much attention you pay to staying in shape, your life is still in God's hand.

He is sovereign—above all. He is the reason you are still on Earth today, still breathing and moving and among the living. It is not because of the health food you ate last night or the two-hour workout you just finished at the gym. God is the Source. He says,

> *...I am the Lord, and I will bring you out from under the burdens of the Egyptians, and I will rid you out of their bondage, and I will redeem you with a stretched out arm...* (Exodus 6:6).

The Hebrew word for *redeem* means "to pluck." Here, God is saying that He will "pluck you out" of that predicament you are in. He will redeem you, "pluck you out," of that trouble, that circumstance that is pressing you, that situation that is beyond your control.

To pluck means "to snatch out of." God will snatch you right out of that bondage. He will snatch you right out of that impossible situation the devil put you in.

That's good news for you who are working in a job that has put you in total bondage. You are about as unhappy as unhappy can be. God can snatch you out of that job that's holding you in bondage and put you in another job where you will experience freedom. How about your relationships? You may be in bondage in your relationships. Perhaps gossip is holding you captive. God hates gossip! He can snatch you out of that situation in which you are being torn apart by gossip. Perhaps you're in bondage to those you are associating with. Maybe you've said, "I'm just going to be in fellowship with a certain type of people." That's bondage. God has an idea of who He wants you to be associated with, and you can't judge by your own standards. You've got to leave room for God to place the relationships He chooses into your life. He can snatch you right out of the wrong kinds of relationships and place you into relationships He has ordained.

He says, "I will redeem you." To redeem also means "to purchase." That's what Jesus did for us on the cross at Calvary: He purchased us. He redeemed us from sin and sickness; from bondage; and from the ultimate bondage, which is eternity in hell. The devil may come at you and tell you, "You're nothing but a pile of junk!" But that's not true. You've been redeemed. You've been purchased at great price by Jesus Christ. It was God's divine plan for you to be saved—redeemed. You may have been a drug pusher, selling drugs on the street corner. You may have felt like you were just a pile of junk. Maybe you were a prostitute and felt worthless, thinking, *What's the use?* You may think you have reason to believe the devil when he reminds you of your past, but it's not true! You're not junk—not if you've been redeemed by the shed blood of Jesus Christ. You can tell the devil to take a hike. And every time he tries to remind you of your past, you can remind him of his future—eternity in the flames of the lake of fire!

Why can you say to the devil, "That's not true! I'm not junk! I've been redeemed"? Because you've been delivered by the hand of God. He delivered you up and out of that mess you were in before you were saved. He delivered you from drugs. He delivered you from prostitution. He delivered you from whoremongering. He delivered you from alcoholism. He delivered you from lying and cheating and running around on your wife. He delivered you from adultery. He delivered you from stealing. To be saved is, simply, to be delivered from the bondage of sin. He delivered you!

So when the devil tries to come at you again and tell you you're not worth a thing, tell him, "That's not true! The Word of God says I am fearfully and wonderfully made [Ps. 139:14]! I've been redeemed—purchased—snatched out of all that stuff I used to be in! Praise God!"

Delivered by His Strength

Our God is strong and mighty. He is a powerful deliverer, full of strength. In Exodus 6:6 He says that He will deliver us "with a stretched out arm, and with great judgments." The term *stretched out arm* in Hebrew means "through the might and power of God." The Lord is saying, "I will stretch you until you are where I want you to be." He is saying, "I will keep right on stretching you with My might and My power by My arm, until you are where you ought to be." In that stretching process is deliverance.

Picture a rubber band: When you hold it in your hand in its relaxed state, it appears to be quite small. Put a little pressure on it and that tiny rubber band expands...and expands, and expands, until it is several times its original length. That's how you may be feeling right now—stretched, under a whole lot of pressure, like you're just about to pop! No, you won't pop. God knows exactly how much pressure to apply in order to get you to where you need to be with Him. He won't stretch you beyond your capacity, nor will He leave you at minimum capacity, for He wants you to reach your maximum potential with Him. He wants you to be all you can be. Only God knows where that point is, so He'll stretch you and stretch you and keep right on stretching you until you get there. That's His hand of deliverance doing all that stretching, and when He's through stretching you, He'll stand back with approval and say, "Well done!"

God wanted the children of God to inherit the promised land, but they were full of fear and unbelief. They had been in Egypt so long that they had become used to bondage. They had an "Egypt" mentality. So God stretched them. He stretched them through the wilderness. He stretched them through adversity. He stretched them through trials and tribulations. He knew their potential, and so He stretched them until they reached it. He did not put more on them than they could handle, nor will He with you.

He will place His yoke upon you in order that you learn of Him. He won't let you break beneath the weight of that yoke because He promises that it is an easy yoke (Mt. 11:30). He is *training* you through that yoke, not trying to break you. Submit to Jesus, and He will stretch you and mold you and shape you—not break you. He'll move you and stretch you and push circumstances and even people out of the way that have been stumbling blocks. He will move whomever and whatever it takes in order to get you to where He wants you to be. In Exodus 6:7-8, He says:

> *...And I will take you to Me for a people, and I will be to you a God: and ye shall know that I am the Lord your God, which bringeth you out from under the burdens of the Egyptians. And I will bring you in unto the land, concerning the which I did swear to give it to Abraham, to Isaac, and to Jacob; and I will give it you for an heritage: I am the Lord.*

In these verses, we see not only the *strength* of our Deliverer but also the *sanctification* of our Deliverer. To be *sanctified* means "to be set apart." It does not mean to wear funny clothes, long dresses, and cover your elbows up at all times and if you're a woman to wear your hair up in a bun and refuse to wear jewelry. No, it means to live set apart. Sanctification is not an outward garment; it is an inward condition of the heart.

There are two forms of sanctification: positional sanctification and practical sanctification.

Positional sanctification is the position God places you in when you are saved. It is yours by inheritance; it is not something that you earn or work your way up to. God places you in the place of positional sanctification. You can't get there on your own; only by the shed blood of Christ.

Practical sanctification is to practice holiness in your daily life. It is this type of sanctification that reflects the day-to-day inward condition of your heart. To practice holiness is an attitude of living that involves everything you do, everything you say, everything you see, everywhere you go, everyone you come in contact with. By walking in holiness, you are making a statement before heaven and earth that you are set apart for a divine purpose, the property of Jesus Christ. God has said, "I will set you apart so that you can know Me and I can know you. And I will be your God. And you shall be My people."

The Guidance of God

The Bible says, "The steps of a good man are ordered by the Lord" (Ps. 37:23b). He promises to guide the steps of the godly; that means He will steer us in the direction we ought to go. He will guide us. He will provide direction and chart our course. He will guide us by the Holy Spirit. He will guide us to our own promised land. Then He will give us our inheritance as He promised to do in Exodus 6. If you want the hand of God's deliverance to be upon you, then just one thing is required of you: Submit to Him. God has already made the way for you. He has already prepared your promised land. He has your inheritance right there waiting for you. Just one thing is required: He needs all of you. He wants *you*! Submit to Him totally; completely; by faith. Then He will deliver you, lead you into the promised land, and give you your inheritance. Just show up. God has everything prearranged. It's ready!

5

God's Hand of Healing

Contrary to some of today's leading theologians, God is still in the business of healing. There are those who don't believe it. However, God said it; I believe it; and that settles it! He's a healing God, the same today as yesterday (see Heb. 13:8). There are modern biblical interpreters who teach that healing passed away, along with the rest of the miracles of the New Testament. They say miracles ended with the Apostolic Era. Now, do I believe that? No way! I don't know what Bible they're using for their interpretation, but mine says God still heals.

And in this study of the hand of God we're going to look at some of those Scriptures.

Jehovah Rapha

Why do I believe so strongly that God is in the healing business today? Because He has revealed Himself as a healing God again and again in the pages of the Bible. Let's look at Exodus 15:26:

>...*If thou wilt diligently hearken to the voice of the Lord thy God, and wilt do that which is right in His sight, and wilt give ear to His commandments, and keep all His statutes, I will put none of these diseases upon thee, which I have brought upon the Egyptians: for I am the Lord that healeth thee.*

In this verse God reveals Himself as Jehovah Rapha, the God who heals. He is God, the Healer. He is saying, "If you walk obediently before Me, I won't afflict you as I have your enemies; I won't let disease come upon you. I am the Lord that healeth thee."

Not only do I believe God heals because the Word says so; I also believe God heals today because of the many existing testimonies to that fact. Multitudes of people currently living around the globe can testify to the healing power of God because they have personally experienced it. People within our present generation have had firsthand knowledge of the healing power of God, and their experiences line up with what the Word says about the God who heals. So, not only are there biblical examples of the healing power of God, but there are also many testimonials to that effect.

If I were in need of healing today, I would first go the Word of God to see what the Lord says about His ability to heal. I would go to the Word and study its contents. I would examine what the Lord said through His prophets. Then I would study what Jesus said about healing. Finally, I would discover what the apostles said about it.

I would wind up with only one revelation: God is a healing God! And because He is the same yesterday, today, and forever (Heb. 13:8), I would have to believe that He heals today...the same as yesterday, and the same as He will heal tomorrow.

Whatever God has done once on earth, He is capable of doing again. The Bible is the written history of God's work, so if we can find it in the Bible, it is available to us today. One hymnist wrote, "It is no secret what God can do; what He's done for others, He'll do for you." That about sums it up. Yet there are those who continually argue that God has stopped healing and performing miracles. If that were true, it would mean that God had changed. And His Word clearly states, "I change not" (see Mal. 3:6). So, if He could heal in the past, He can heal now. And He does!

God's Ability to Heal

One of my favorite biblical examples of God's ability to heal is the story of the healing of Naaman, the Leper, found in Second Kings.

Now Naaman, captain of the host of the king of Syria, was a great man with his master, and honourable, because by him the Lord had given deliverance unto Syria: he was also a mighty man in valour, but he was a leper. And the Syrians had gone out by companies, and had brought away captive out of the land of Israel a little maid; and she waited on Naaman's wife. And she said unto her mistress, Would God my lord were with the prophet that is in Samaria! for he would recover him of his leprosy. And one went in, and told his lord, saying, Thus and thus said the maid that is of the land of Israel (2 Kings 5:1-4).

Here is what the Lord showed me as I read this passage of text: I saw that Naaman had *captured his cure* without even realizing it! The answer to his healing was within his own household—the little maid who served his wife. In understanding this, we can see just how the healing hand of God works—in mysterious ways!

Here was Naaman, a great warrior, a mighty man of valor, and a leper; outcast by society, feared and avoided. The Scriptures state the Lord had used him as an instrument of deliverance for Syria. Here was a great man of war, a courageous fighter, a respected leader, victorious because the Lord had used him to win Syria's freedom. Yet he was unable to hide the fact that he was stricken with leprosy—the most dreaded of all diseases in the ancient Middle East.

But God was there ahead of Naaman with His healing hand stretched out. Naaman captured a little maid of Israel and took her into his own household as a servant to his wife. That little maid had knowledge of a prophet in Israel who was known to heal leprosy. There was Naaman's answer—right there, waiting for him!

God has a way of fulfilling His purposes in our lives—often in mysterious ways, as was the case with Naaman. He orchestrates many things so He will receive the complete glory.

Naaman had captured his own cure and didn't even know it! The answer was right there in plain sight, and he might have missed it, had he not listened to those who overheard the maid's remarks about the prophet of Israel and reported to Naaman what they had heard. It seemed so simple: Go to Israel and find the prophet! The nature of man is to look for the very complex when the answer is so simple it's in plain sight! And Naaman was looking for something big and dynamic—a cure to his leprosy, which was well-known to be incurable.

What could this little maid know about healing leprosy? She was totally insignificant—just a servant to his wife. She was unimportant, nothing but a slave. It would have been very easy for Naaman to ignore her claims of the supernatural power of God that moved through the prophet of Israel.

Here she was, a nobody, making rash claims: "I believe the master can be healed if he'll just seek out the prophet!" Who would expect Naaman to listen to a nobody? Yet God used this little maid whose name is not even recorded in Scripture to deliver a divine suggestion to the mighty warrior, Naaman. Something about that divine suggestion leapt forth and brought hope to Naaman's downcast spirit. Could it be that this maid told the truth?

So Naaman petitioned the king of Syria to send a letter to the king of Israel, and lavish gifts accompanied the letter:

And the king of Syria said, Go to, go, and I will send a letter unto the king of Israel. And he departed, and took with him ten talents of silver, and six thousand pieces of gold, and ten changes of raiment. And he brought the letter to the king of Israel, saying, Now when this letter is come unto thee, behold, I have therewith sent Naaman my servant to thee, that thou mayest recover him of his leprosy. And it came to pass, when the king of Israel had read the letter, that he rent his clothes, and said, Am I God, to kill and to make alive, that this man doth send unto me to recover a man of his leprosy? Wherefore consider, I pray you, and see how he seeketh a quarrel against me. And it was so, when Elisha the man of God had heard that the king of Israel had rent his clothes, that he sent to the king, saying, Wherefore hast thou rent thy clothes? Let him come now to me, and he shall know that there is a prophet in Israel (2 Kings 5:5-8).

Naaman went straight to the top, petitioning the king of Syria to intercede on his behalf with the king of Israel, yet all along he was in need of the man of God—Elisha. The king of Israel knew immediately that he had no power to secure Naaman's healing, so political means were obviously not the answer. Naaman needed a miracle, and when Elisha heard of his condition, he said, "Come!"

The first thing you need to understand from these verses is that divine healing cannot be purchased. It's not for sale! You can't pay some TV evangelist a big "donation" and get healed. If somebody states, "If you send me…" turn the TV off! Shut it off! If anyone ever states, "If you send me X number of dollars, I'll pray, and you'll be healed," channel surf right on out of there. Healing is from the hand of God, and it's not for sale.

A number of years ago, I visited my aunt and found that she had pinned a little piece of cloth beneath her pillow. When I asked her what it was, she said a televangelist had sent it to her, along with the promise that if she put it in her Bible, then under the pillow, she would be healed. I asked, "How much did you send him?" She said, "I've been sending him 'such and such amount' regularly." She wasn't healed; it was all hype. She died of a brain tumor. If anyone ever indicates to you that they can heal you for a price, get out of there fast. God's healing power is free for the asking.

Naaman thought if he brought silver and gold and fine clothing to the prophet, it would win him favor and perhaps even secure his healing. Naaman discovered immediately that divine healing was not for sale—certainly not from Elisha. The prophet of God was not impressed with Naaman's stature or accomplishments; he was not moved by his lavish gifts.

So Naaman came with his horses and with his chariot, and stood at the door of the house of Elisha. And Elisha sent a messenger unto him, saying, Go and wash in Jordan seven times, and thy flesh shall come again to thee, and thou shalt be clean. But Naaman was wroth, and went away, and said, Behold, I thought, He will surely come out to me, and stand, and call on the name of the Lord his God, and strike his hand over the place, and recover the leper. Are not Abana and Pharpar, rivers of Damascus, better than all the waters of Israel? may I not wash in them, and be clean? So he turned and went away in a rage (2 Kings 5:9-12).

Naaman almost missed receiving his healing. He was so lifted up with pride and so taken with who he was and with his station in life that he was deeply offended when Elisha would not even meet with him face to face, but instead sent instructions through a messenger! And the message was clear: "Naaman, all your money, all your power, all your influence mean nothing here. To be healed, you're going to have to humble yourself before the mighty hand of God." God was not impressed with Naaman, nor was Elisha. Naaman left the prophet's house in a rage.

Yet it was God's will to heal Naaman's leprosy. Healing had been made available to him. The instructions were clear: Dip seven times in the river Jordan. Immediately, Naaman began to reason: *Why Jordan? It's filthy! We have better rivers in Damascus. I'll wash there.* And if Naaman had stopped there, he would have missed God, because it's the anointing that breaks the yoke—not the river you dip in. It was the anointing that brought God's power to heal, not Naaman's stature or Elisha's human abilities. The hand of God rested upon the prophet, and God anointed Elisha's instructions for Naaman's healing. Elisha didn't even have to lay hands on Naaman in order for him to receive healing.

God is the Source of our healing today, the same as in Naaman's day. Always remember that. Don't run across town to follow some man just because he says he's a healer. God is the Healer! Never forget that. Always check the anointing. And remember, it's not for sale.

The Foolish Things

God often uses the foolish things on earth to confound the wise. Here was the mighty Naaman being told to go for a swim in Jordan and dunk himself seven times. How foolish! But the Lord dealt with him in the midst of his rage, and through his servants, Naaman was convinced to obey the prophet after all. He did as he was told, and miraculously, Naaman was healed. (See 2 Kings 5:13-15.)

The prophet had said, "Send him to me!" And God intervened for Naaman.

There is also the story of the woman in Zarephath, whose son had died. She sent for the prophet Elijah, who said, "Give him to me." Divine intervention! He said, in essence, "You can't handle this situation. You're losing your cool, losing your faith. Give this situation to me!" (See 1 Kings 17:19.) The prophet laid down on the boy and breathed on him until life returned to his small body. Foolish! But the boy was healed.

Then there is the story of how Jesus healed a man's lunatic son who had continually cast himself down on the ground and into the fire. This boy had seizures that put his life in jeopardy and caused him to become branded as crazy. Everyone had tried to heal this boy, but without success. In Matthew, chapter 17, Jesus stood up and said, "Give him to Me!" The boy was healed instantly.

There are those today who continue to place their trust for their healing in secular sources. They place their confidence in the wise things, not the foolish things.

They place their trust in the medical community and in the ministry of their deacons, who pray over them and send them away unhealed. I'm not saying you should not go to doctors; nor am I telling you not to have your deacons lay hands on you and pray. I am saying, "Trust God! He is your Healer!" Don't give up on your healing until you hear from God. He always has the last word.

The Lord Tests Our Sincerity

Here is something you need to know about healing: Before you receive it, God will test your sincerity. Yes, God tests the sincerity of those who seek His healing hand. There are folks who constantly holler for healing, saying they want to be delivered. But they have their own agenda and preconceived notion of how, when, and where they'll receive it. They have already decided how they want it to happen. Then when they don't get it, they're amazed. But God is saying, "Let's see how badly you want it. Let's see if you really want to graduate. How badly do you want to be healed? Badly enough to hang in there and let Me do it My way? Badly enough to allow Me to use the foolish things to confound the wise?"

That's why Naaman was so confounded when Elisha sent his messenger out to deliver his instructions. Naaman thought he was a big-shot who deserved a personal audience with the prophet. Not so! God was testing his sincerity. How badly did Naaman actually want to be healed? The mighty warrior stomped off in a rage, muttering, "He didn't even come out of the house! I can't believe it! Doesn't Elisha know who I am? At least he could have acknowledged me enough to come outside and meet me. I thought he'd at least come out and lay hands on me."

But that's not how God chose to operate through Elisha in Naaman's case. Here was a leper whose disease could not be hid. It was obvious to all that regardless of his many accomplishments in battle, regardless of his many medals of honor for valor on the firing line, Naaman was a social outcast, stricken with a horrible disease that would eventually cause his body to rot away beyond recognition.

Naaman was looking for some big, dynamic sign or wonder, such as thunder and lightning, to signify his healing had indeed come. Instead, he received simple instructions to bathe in the Jordan, and from a messenger! But when God anoints, even simple instructions become divinely infused with power to heal and deliver. Here, God was saying to Naaman, "How badly do you want to be healed? Badly enough to obey foolish instructions and go for a swim in a dirty river?"

Naaman's servants knew the warrior had a lot on the line. What if the prophet's instructions would work? What did the mighty Naaman have to lose?

To obey those instructions would mean Naaman would have to humble himself before God and man. He would have to come down from his lofty position long enough to bathe publicly in a dirty river like some common peasant. He would have to dip himself beneath the waters of Jordan, not just once, but seven times. Whoever heard of such a thing as dipping in dirty water seven times to become *clean*?

But here's a word for today: If you want God to heal you, He'll have to do it His way. If you are going to receive His healing today, you'll have to follow His instructions, just as Naaman did. Don't try to shortchange God by giving Him two prayers and then expecting miracles. Do whatever He tells you; *then* expect miracles.

Many miss their blessings because they won't do what God tells them to do. If He says, "Hearken diligently unto Me," then believe it and do it. Why? Because He is the God that "healeth thee" (Ex. 15:26b).

Naaman would have missed it totally if he had failed to hearken to his servants who told him what the little maid had said. But he chose to listen, and he traveled all the way to Israel to find the prophet, Elisha. Then he almost blew it by getting angry and refusing to do what the prophet had said. Fortunately, his servants spoke boldly:

And his servants came near, and spake unto him, and said, My father, if the prophet had bid thee do some great thing, wouldest thou not have done it? how much rather then, when he saith to thee, Wash, and be clean? Then went he down, and dipped himself seven times in Jordan, according to the saying of the man of God: and his flesh came again like unto the flesh of a little child, and he was clean (2 Kings 5:13-14).

Naaman's servants said, "The bottom line is this: You've got leprosy. You're going to die anyway. You've come this far in search of healing. What do you have to lose by doing what the prophet says to do? You can't even move about the land freely. You have leprosy; your movements are restricted. There are some places that are totally off limits to you. You've been isolated; you've been ostracized; you've been criticized; you've been feared and abhorred. Things can't get any worse. Why not trust God and go for that swim?"

It's God's way or no way. If you will be healed, it will be on His terms and His terms only. It takes humility to receive healing on those terms.

Naaman obeyed the man of God and was healed.

But not everyone who says he's a man of God is actually a man of God. Not everyone who wears a clergy collar has been sent by God; nor is he necessarily anointed. Everyone who knows enough Scripture to quote it is not necessarily a Bible-believing, anointed man of God. You'd better know he's a man of God before you go dipping yourself into something that you can't get out of. Make sure of who he is before you obey his instructions, because you can't judge a man of God by the robes he wears. You can judge him just one way: by his fruit.

When he tells you something, check it out in the Book. Does it line up with the Word? Just a word of warning: Check the fruit.

Changed by Divine Encounter

Now, watch how divine healing increases our knowledge of the divine nature of God:

And he returned to the man of God, he and all his company, and came, and stood before him: and he said, Behold, now I know that there is no God in all the earth,

*but in Israel: now therefore, I pray thee, take a blessing
of thy servant* (2 Kings 5:15).

Five minutes before this, Naaman had no idea who
God was. Five minutes before, he had been covered with
leprous boils and filled with rage, refusing to dip himself
in the river Jordan. But now that he had obeyed the man
of God, Naaman was filled with the knowledge of God.
He had been touched by God's healing hand, and he was
filled with awe and thanksgiving for the Lord Most High.

Something happens when you have a personal encounter with God. Something happens when you have a
divine encounter. Something happens in your life when
God does something that had previously seemed impossible. You are changed by these encounters. When the
hand of God touches you, you are forever changed.

Naaman received his healing and immediately returned to the prophet to testify. He praised God, then
offered to bestow costly gifts upon the servant of the
Lord. But Elisha wisely refused. Otherwise, it would have
seemed that one could, indeed, "buy" healing.

You can't buy a blessing. You can't buy healing. You
can't buy miracles. Keep your gifts in your pockets.
There is no way you can pay for what God has done in
your life. All you must do is testify about it later. Tell
somebody about the goodness of God. Tell somebody
that God still heals—today! He is Jehovah Rapha, the
God who healeth thee!

6

God's Hand of Discipline

And ye have forgotten the exhortation which speaketh unto you as unto children, My son, despise not thou the chastening of the Lord, nor faint when thou art rebuked of Him: For whom the Lord loveth He chasteneth, and scourgeth every son whom He receiveth. If ye endure chastening, God dealeth with you as with sons; for what son is he whom the father chasteneth not? But if ye be without chastisement, whereof all are partakers, then are ye bastards, and not sons. Furthermore we have had fathers of our flesh which corrected us, and we gave them reverence: shall we not much rather be in subjection unto the Father of spirits, and live? For they verily for a few days chastened us after their own pleasure; but He for our profit, that we might be partakers of His holiness. Now no chastening for the present seemeth to be joyous, but grievous: nevertheless afterward it yieldeth the peaceable fruit of righteousness unto them which are exercised thereby (Hebrews 12:5-11).

God's hand of discipline; it's very important to understand this facet of the hand of God. This is no passage of Scripture to play with. It's part of how God trains us and deals with us as His children. No one understands the concept of parenting better than Him. He knows just what we need in the way of chastisement. He knows just how much chastisement we need and for how long. God, after all, is the essence of what parenthood is all about. Who knows child rearing better than He? He is the divine Role Model.

The term *chastisement* as used in Hebrews, chapter 12, means simply "discipline." But there are some things we must look at in order to understand God's hand of discipline. First, we must know that chastisement—discipline—is to be encouraged. No one enjoys being disciplined. Yet the discipline is necessary in order for us to grow and mature as God's children.

We are familiar with Scripture verses elsewhere in the Bible that deal with the Lord's chastisement. Proverbs 3:5-6 states, "Trust in the Lord with all thine heart; and lean not unto thine own understanding. In all thy ways acknowledge Him, and He shall direct thy paths." This sounds nice. But how does He direct our paths? As we read on in the same chapter, we encounter verses 11 and 12, which are not as "reader-friendly":

My son, despise not the chastening of the Lord; neither be weary of His correction: For whom the Lord loveth He correcteth; even as a father the son in whom he delighteth (Proverbs 3:11-12).

Again, we see that the chastening of the Lord is not to be despised, but embraced as something for our own ultimate good.

Discipline is to be encouraged. I don't care what you hear on television about the world's disdain for discipline; God says it is to be encouraged. Everyone needs chastening from time to time. It's for our good, not our harm. Yet everywhere around us society discourages disciplinary action. That's one of the reasons the world is so messed up. It's why thieves feel free to break into our houses and steal what we've worked hard to buy. People have no respect for one another and have not been properly disciplined, so they lie and steal and commit violent crimes.

For believers, discipline should be expected. It's part of the package. When God says, "Despise not the chastening of the Lord," He's saying, "It's good for you!" The words *despise not* simply mean "don't take lightly," or "don't think little of." So we are to respect and revere the chastening of the Lord; pay attention to it; learn from it.

Consider these facts: We are living on a planet that we did not create. We breathe air that is here for our use, but even our very breathing we do not control. We stand on ground we did not structure and then think the world is unfair because we can't always have our own way. This ain't Burger King! We can't always have it our way! We're never too old to learn, and that involves the discipline of God. God says we are to despise not the chastening of the Lord when it comes, and it will surely come.

When it does, we are to "faint not." In other words, we are told, "Don't lose heart when the chastening comes, when you are rebuked by God." The word *rebuked* in the Greek means "to convict." So this passage is saying, "Don't lose heart when you are convicted."

Discipline does not necessarily mean to be beaten. God doesn't always take a switch or a belt after us. Sometimes His punishment takes on subtler forms—kind of like when we put our kids on probation for bringing home a bad report card. We don't whip them; however, we deal firmly with them for a period of time.

You and I ought to expect to go through times of the Lord's chastisement. We ought to expect God to take some form of action with us, some disciplinary action. We ought to also come to the understanding that the discipline of the Lord is an expression of His love. Look at Hebrews 12:6:

For whom the Lord loveth He chasteneth, and scourgeth every son whom He receiveth.

Discipline is an expression of God's love. I know that may not seem to make sense, but that's what the Word says. We should endeavor to understand it from that perspective. As parents, we have time and again told our children while we were disciplining them, "This is for your own good!" That's how it is with God's discipline: It's for our good. It's for our training. It's for our correction. It's for our ultimate benefit.

When I was a child, it didn't make any sense to me when my mom and dad told me, "This is for your own good." As a child, I viewed discipline with extreme distaste and did everything I could to avoid going through it. That's because I didn't understand what discipline was about. When I became a parent, I understood more clearly that in order to raise my kids to live godly lives, discipline was going to be required from time to time.

There are people today who carry around negative attitudes toward God because He has been instructing them in certain areas—disciplining them—and they are fighting Him. They get wrong attitudes and think God doesn't love them anymore. They ask, "Why is this happening to me? How come I have to go through this? Why can't somebody else go through this instead of me? Why am I experiencing this thing?"

The reason they don't understand the discipline of God is that they are spiritually immature. When a person grows in God, he comes to understand that God's love doesn't always mean God will give him what he wants, how he wants it, when he wants it, the way he wants it. God also takes disciplinary action in order to express His love. It's not that God has an attitude; it's not because He's mad. It's because He's God. He sees everything perfectly. He sees what's best. He's not about to spoil His children rotten.

Some folks get angry with me because I believe in discipline in the house of God. You can't just enter a church and do what you want because you've paid your money. Paying your tithes is just your duty; you're not really giving anything more than that which is required of you in the Word of God. Paying tithes does not give a person permission to do whatever he wants to do once he is in church. It doesn't give a person the right to talk to the pastor in a disrespectful way. No, discipline is required.

You can't go out into the world and do whatever you want and get by with it; neither can you do whatever you want in the house of God. Discipline is required in the world and in church. And when it comes, it's not because God hates you. It's because He loves you and wants to train you correctly. Love is not letting you do whatever you want to do; it's keeping you from doing that which is harmful to you and others. So to be disciplined by God is not to have some rope tied around your neck, spiritually speaking. It is to be restrained by Him. Perhaps you began to attack the leadership, the elders, or the prophets of God. The Word says not to do that. You were about to hang yourself with your own rope. Instead of allowing that to happen, God steps in and chastens you—for your good. Because He loves you, He'll keep you from committing spiritual suicide.

When it's time for the chastening of God, you can't pick your punishment. No, the choice is not up to you. There is no choice if He's in charge. Whatever God says goes, and there's no negotiating. Sometimes the punishment is less severe, and sometimes it's an actual beating.

For whom the Lord loveth He chasteneth, and scourgeth every son whom He receiveth (Hebrews 12:6).

Society says spanking causes personality disorders in children. But that's not what the Word says. It says that if we spare the rod, we hate our child (see Prov. 13:24). Discipline, then, begins from the cradle. And because we are His children, it will continue to our grave.

Train Up a Child

There are those in society today who don't believe in applying the rod. They'll call children's services if you even attempt to spank a kid in public school. I want my kids disciplined. In fact, I've told my kids that if they're disrespectful to their mother and me, they can count on a spanking. They can expect it. When they talk to us, they'd better do it respectfully or they'll be disciplined. I want my kids to know the power of the rod of correction. I have discovered that disciplinary action should not be postponed. When a child acts in such a way as to require disciplinary action, it should be done immediately, in a manner befitting the situation, to achieve maximum results.

Proverbs 22:15 is explicit in telling us: "Foolishness is bound in the heart of a child; but the rod of correction shall drive it far from him." Again, we see good results from the rod of correction being applied at the appropriate time. Glory to God! Look what the Word says: Foolishness may be there in a child's heart, but you can expel it through loving discipline. Start disciplining your children early enough. Don't wait until there are already huge problems.

Now look at Proverbs 23:13-14:

Withhold not correction from the child: for if thou beatest him with the rod, he shall not die. Thou shalt beat him with the rod, and shalt deliver his soul from hell.

If you break a child's rebellion now, applying the right amount of judicious discipline and correction, the police won't have to break him of it later. That's the bottom line. You're training that child for a law-abiding life in a society that has become crooked, corrupt, and filled with opportunities to go astray. What's it going to be? Spank him now or see him spend time in jail later? Send him to his room now and take away some privileges, or visit him in the slammer later? Make him do his homework now and punish him if he doesn't, or sit by helplessly later when he comes home from school and informs you that he's just dropped out for good? Make him sit down at the dinner table and eat correctly, talk correctly, and use the right table manners, or later he will learn to walk all over you, curse you to your face, and call you by your first name instead of a respectful "Mom" and "Dad." No, there's no question as far as I'm concerned. I'm going to discipline my kids according to the guidelines established in the Word of God. That's just how it's gonna be.

If you think back in light of what the Word says, the punishment you received from your parents was not because they hated you, but because they loved you. Because they loved you, they trained you. They applied the rod of correction on your bottom for your own good.

Not only is God's correction a sign of His love expressed to us, but discipline should also be endured.

Don't run from God's chastening; endure it. That's what the Word says: "If ye endure chastening, God dealeth with you as with sons; for what son is he whom the father chasteneth not?" (Heb. 12:7) That word *endure* means "to stay" or "to remain up under" that form of discipline being meted out to you. Endure it! Stay under it. Don't run from it. Let it perform its work in your life.

There are those who tell their kids, "As long as you're in my house, you'll do as I say!" But I tell my kids, "As long as you're alive, I'm your daddy and you will respect me. It has nothing to do with when you leave this house; this is a lifetime arrangement. You'll never be too old to respect me, and you'll never be too old for me to express my opinions in certain situations. If you don't want my opinion, don't call me and don't ask for it." That's how I was raised, by the way. One day I thought I was big enough to tell my daddy what I thought, man to man, and he told me, "Wait a minute, boy! You don't ever get too old to respect your elders!" Daddy had the last word that day, and that was the end of that. It doesn't matter how old your children get, you are still due their respect.

But respect for authority works two ways: When you respect the proper lines of authority in your life, you are in line for the blessings of God. You are in a fantastic position with God to be blessed by your Father in heaven. The word *father* as it is found in Hebrews, chapter 12, means "protector, provider, and upholder." God is your Protector. He is your Provider. He is your Upholder. As your Father, He wants only that which is best for you, and sometimes He will need to correct your current course in order for you to be able to receive His best for you.

Even as a grown man, I feel secure in the company of my parents. But I really feel protected when I'm in the company of my daddy. Even though I'm an adult with children of my own, I feel safe when I'm with my dad. I feel more secure with him than with anyone else on earth. I want my kids to be able to one day say that about me.

I remember a time when my children were small that I called home to check on things during a break in a meeting with the board of deacons. At home, it was thundering and raining, and my wife told me the weather was so turbulent that the children were afraid. I said, "Well, give them the phone." I talked to each of the children and told them that everything was going to be okay. They listened to my voice and instantly became calm. Just the sound of my voice made them feel safer. By the time I got home, the storm had passed and the children felt safe because daddy was home. That's how it is with God; we should always feel safe with Him because we are under His authority, His covering, His protection.

So not only should discipline be endured, but we should also not try to exclude ourselves from it. Hebrews 12:8 says, "But if ye be without chastisement, whereof all are partakers, then are ye bastards, and not sons." If we exclude ourselves from the chastisement of the Lord, then we are putting ourselves into an illegitimate status with Him. If we stay under God's chastisement and endure His discipline, then He will treat us like His own sons.

We are adopted into the Kingdom through the finished work of Christ. He purchased our adoption papers on the cross at Calvary. We need to stay under the covering of those adoption papers, not go out on our own and try to have it our way.

Furthermore, discipline should be embraced. We should prefer it to going our own way. Here is what Hebrews 12:9-10 states:

Furthermore we have had fathers of our flesh which corrected us, and we gave them reverence: shall we not much rather be in subjection unto the Father of spirits, and live? For they verily for a few days chastened us after their own pleasure; but He for our profit, that we might be partakers of His holiness.

It is for our enhancement that we are being disciplined. It is to our advantage that we endure it and receive the reward in us that it produces. Discipline will produce edified disciples.

Now no chastening for the present seemeth to be joyous, but grievous: nevertheless afterward it yieldeth the peaceable fruit of righteousness unto them which are exercised thereby (Hebrews 12:11).

God's disciplinary action produces fruit in our lives. It will produce a harvest of peace and righteousness. It will help us to live right, holy lives before God. It will train us correctly and produce good fruit for the future. And in order to live for Christ, everyone must go through this training program.

God's training program begins when the trainee begins a healthy, well-balanced diet. We must eat right. We must eat the Bread of Life daily—no need to put butter on it, no need to sweeten it up. It will feed us, just the way it is—the way God ordained it. Then when the Holy Ghost helps us to digest it, He'll mix a little heat with it until the Word of God begins to burn away the fat. That's Holy Ghost exercise; you don't need a Stairmaster for this kind of spiritual exercise program!

Then you get on the treadmill of trials and tribulations and work out awhile longer. Remember, you're in training camp. The Bible says it's good for you, so stay with it. Don't faint in the midst of those trials. You won't be spiritually fit unless they come and you learn to endure and walk patiently onward. Then you'll have to do some spiritual sit-ups to tighten up your inner man with practical sanctification. All these spiritual exercises will help you to become the kind of believer you need to be.

Finally, you'll have to do some pushups to strengthen your arms, so you can bear up under your daily struggles. You may be having problems carrying your burdens. Just start doing some daily spiritual pushups—with your hands lifted up to God in praise. The devil may be trying to hold you down and steal your joy, but praise to God will put the devil in his place. Pull up on praise. You'll feel those burdens lifting soon. Finally, the best exercise of all takes place on bended knee. Those knee-bends are called prayer. Humble yourself before the Lord in prayer and you'll discover that although you went down on your knees with a burden, you rose to your feet with a blessing. You went down a victim and came up a victor. Hallelujah! The Lord will strengthen you in prayer and turn your troubles into triumph.

Keep on lifting those weights; keep on pumping that iron with those spiritual exercises; and soon enough you will find yourself beefed up—disciplined—transformed by God into a healthy, strong believer.

7

God's Hand of Judgment

In the Old Testament, we see the term *Baal* again and again. Just what is "Baal"? Baal is an idol, the worship of which is idolatry, and there are even today many Baals in this world. People today, as in ancient times, still consult the Baals of this world for answers. In so doing, they are bringing down the hand of God's judgment upon their lives.

What are some of these modern-day Baals? Psychics. Astrology. The signs of the Zodiac. The New Age. Lady Luck. Good-luck charms. Crystals. Horoscopes. There are those who call themselves Christians, yet will read their daily horoscopes before they open their Bibles. Then they wonder why God isn't blessing their lives. They are canceling out their ability to receive blessing by consulting Baals. Baals don't mix with the things of God. It must be one or the other, but not both.

So the Baals must come down! We must go up to the high places of our daily lives and topple the Baals. We

---

must bring them down and keep them down because God and only God shall be exalted. Only He shall we worship. That is not by suggestion, but by command—the First Commandment!

We were made in the image of God. That means only one thing: We were made in His likeness. It does not mean we will ever be *like* God. Nowhere within fallen man is the capacity to become *like God*. No, that's Baal worship. All this attention to self-esteem and self-image is just another form of it. We are not to exalt ourselves; we are to exalt God. Only God shall be worshiped. The Bible is very specific about that.

People today, as in the days of old, are consulting Baals. They are putting their trust in Elijah Muhammad. They are putting their trust in Louis Farrakhan. They are putting their trust in local, state, and national governments. They are putting their trust in the White House, which is the wrong house; because when all is said and done, only God's house will be left standing.

So, in order for the people of God to get to where they ought to be in Him, they will have to stop putting their trust in all these empty dreams and nonessentials. They must take a long, hard look at their lives and go after the Baals they have allowed to coexist with the things of God. Those Baals have been killing off their blessings, and it's time to do something about it before God's hand of judgment comes upon them with a hard lesson.

God Is On the Move

I believe God is up to something on the earth today. I believe He is going to send the rain of righteousness that

will flood the earth. But in order for Him to move might-
ily in that way, all those Baals must come down. We have
to start identifying them, naming them, and pulling
them down—then throw them away—in order for the
next move of God to take place.

Wherever the hand of the Lord is found in Scripture,
there is power. It means God is in control. So let's set the
stage to study the pulling down of modern-day Baals by
looking at Israel during the reign of the weak King Ahab
and his wicked queen, Jezebel. All Israel feared this
woman, primarily because she consulted Baals. Her
priests consulted demon spirits and worshiped idols.
Look at what First Kings says about her influence on
King Ahab:

> *And he reared up an altar for Baal in the house of Baal,*
> *which he had built in Samaria. And Ahab made a*
> *grove; and Ahab did more to provoke the Lord God of Is-*
> *rael to anger than all the kings of Israel that were before*
> *him* (1 Kings 16:32-33).

This guy was wicked! All kinds of perverse things
went on in the house of Baal in the course of their worship practices, including sexual orgies. Temple prostitution took place, as well as frenzied dancing culminating
with the sexual act. Whoremongering, homosexuality—
every form of perversion took place in the course of this
evil idol worship. This pagan worship was sanctioned
and participated in by the king of Israel, one who had
been chosen by God to fulfill that office. Ahab got
caught up in idol worship and God became so angry that

He took measures against all Israel. According to First Kings 17, He sent a famine:

And Elijah the Tishbite, who was of the inhabitants of Gilead, said unto Ahab, As the Lord God of Israel liveth, before whom I stand, there shall not be dew nor rain these years, but according to my word. And the word of the Lord came unto him, saying, Get thee hence, and turn thee eastward, and hide thyself by the brook Cherith, that is before Jordan. And it shall be, that thou shalt drink of the brook; and I have commanded the ravens to feed thee there (1 Kings 17:1-4).

God was fed up! God's grace completely ran out for Ahab and for all Israel. Famine meant no rain, no crops. Nothing would grow; there would be no production. The land dried up. And there was no water. Without water, all living things—all vegetation, all cattle, all sheep—would die, and eventually so would the people. No one can live for very long without water. That's why the Lord directed the prophet Elijah to go to the Brook Cherith, where there would be a supply of water to keep his body from dehydrating.

Even in the midst of famine, God's man, Elijah, was still able to see the hand of the Lord. Even in the midst of trouble on every side, God's hand was there to guide and protect him. The Lord led him to the town of Zarephath, where a widow sustained him with her supply of meal and cruse of oil that miraculously lasted them both throughout the famine!

It was the hand of God that brought the famine, and, as we'll see in chapter 18 of First Kings, it was the hand of God that stopped it; but not until the Baals had been sufficiently dealt with in the land of Israel.

The Baals Must Come Down!

Everyone wanted the famine to cease. But that's just the way people are. They want it easy. They don't want to have to change. They want miracles without making a few necessary adjustments. It's been that way throughout history. The people of Israel wanted rain. And they finally got it—after the land was cleansed of Baal worship.

And it came to pass after many days, that the word of the Lord came to Elijah in the third year, saying, Go, shew thyself unto Ahab; and I will send rain upon the earth. And Elijah went to shew himself unto Ahab. And there was a sore famine in Samaria. And Ahab called Obadiah, which was the governor of his house. (Now Obadiah feared the Lord greatly: For it was so, when Jezebel cut off the prophets of the Lord, that Obadiah took an hundred prophets, and hid them by fifty in a cave, and fed them with bread and water.) And Ahab said unto Obadiah, Go into the land, unto all fountains of water, and unto all brooks, peradventure we may find grass to save the horses and mules alive, that we lose not all the beasts. So they divided the land between them to pass throughout it: Ahab went one way by himself, and Obadiah went another way by himself. And as Obadiah was in the way, behold, Elijah met him: and he knew him, and fell on his face, and said, Art thou that my lord Elijah? And he answered him, I am: go, tell thy lord, Behold, Elijah is here. And he said, What have I sinned, that thou wouldest deliver thy servant into the hand of Ahab, to slay me? As the Lord thy God liveth, there is no nation or kingdom, whither my lord hath not sent to seek thee; and when they said, He is not there; he took an oath of the kingdom and nation, that they found thee not. And now thy sayest, Go, tell thy lord, Behold, Elijah is here (1 Kings 18:1-11).

It was terrible throughout the land; everything was dry and dying. Ahab was in search of a little water to save his livestock. So he sent Obadiah to search for water. Instead, Obadiah found Elijah, a wanted man. Ahab had put a price on his head. Now the prophet was demanding, "Tell Ahab I am here! Tell him I have a word for him from the Lord."

That struck fear in the heart of Obadiah, who knew the hand of God rested on Elijah in a powerful way. And he did as he was told to do.

And it came to pass, when Ahab saw Elijah, that Ahab said unto him, Art thou he that troubleth Israel? And he answered, I have not troubled Israel; but thou, and thy father's house, in that ye have forsaken the commandments of the Lord, and thou hast followed Baalim (1 Kings 18:17-18).

How easy it is to blame someone or something other than to accept responsibility for our own actions! Ahab was trying to turn the whole thing around on Elijah and blame him for the famine, when in fact the famine was a direct result of the sins of the house of Ahab.

Modern-Day Baals

That's still a problem today. We want to blame our trouble on something other than ourselves. We have a form of godliness in this nation of ours, while we deny the power thereof. We have just enough religion in the land to make things look good from the outside. Yet we allow gambling, lotteries, and organized crime to prosper, and we warehouse criminals through our justice system.

Sometimes God has to whip us into line. That's when He chastens us and allows some type of personal famine to hit our lives so we will examine ourselves before Him, turn to Him, repent, and make some changes.

You know how it goes: You promise God that if He'll just help you with the bills, you'll become a tither. Then He helps you, and you forget the promise you just made about tithing. Or perhaps you say, "Lord, if You just help me put my child through college, I'll get involved in church ministry. I'll serve You. I promise!" Then He helps you, and you forget your promise to Him when it comes time to fulfill it. But God keeps right on delivering you and helping you, even though each time afterward you run right back to Baal.One day He may bring some discipline to situations like these.

A Spiritual Famine

Ahab's problem was not a famine in the land; his problem was that he had turned away from God. Thus, the people of Israel followed his leadership and turned away from God too. It was Ahab who was being held responsible for this gross departure from the right path. And the entire land suffered the hand of God's judgment.

Believe me: Baals will bring the hand of God's judgment. Psychics, horoscopes, Jehovah's Witnesses, Buddhism, the New Age, Christian Science, Elijah Muhammad, Louis Farrakhan—that stuff will bring on the hand of God's judgment. He will turn His hand upon you until you turn from those things and repent and begin to serve Him once more with your whole heart.

Look at these verses:

And the children of Israel did evil in the sight of the Lord, and served Baalim: And they forsook the Lord God of their fathers, which brought them out of the land of Egypt, and followed other gods, of the gods of the people that were round about them, and bowed themselves unto them, and provoked the Lord to anger (Judges 2:11-12).

What was the result of the people serving other gods? God became angered against them.

We see the same result today when people stray from the Lord and begin to serve other gods. Why is it that people would rather serve a god of their own creation than serve the God of all creation? That's easy enough to answer: They think they can control the gods of their own making. This attitude will provoke God's anger.

What does it mean to *provoke*? That word means "to challenge," or "to goad." When we were kids we used to provoke fights by jabbing someone in the ribs, push-ing them, or chanting things like, "I double-dare you!" That's what the children of Israel did when they began to serve the Baals around them instead of the God of their fathers. They provoked God to anger.

And they forsook the Lord, and served Baal and Ash-taroth. And the anger of the Lord was hot against Israel, and He delivered them into the hands of spoilers that spoiled them, and He sold them into the hands of their enemies round about, so that they could not any longer stand before their enemies. Whithersoever they went out, the hand of the Lord was against them for evil, as the Lord had said, and as the Lord had sworn unto them: and they were greatly distressed (Judges 2:13-15).

According to these verses, God's punishment was to deliver the people into the hands of their enemies. Any favor they had previously experienced from God was on hold—at least, temporarily. The hand of the Lord was against them, and that would continue to be the case un-til the people repented, turned away from the Baals, turned back toward God, and destroyed the idols they had allowed to come between them and their relation-ship with the Lord.

Any time a person chooses to serve false gods, the hand of the Lord is against them. I don't care what year it is, or what period in history. Idol worship is idol wor-ship, and the punishment is always the same.

Elijah and the Prophets of Baal

Elijah called a meeting on the top of Mount Carmel and invited all the prophets of Baal who had flocked into

Israel under the leadership of King Ahab and Queen Jezebel. Hundreds of them came to engage in a battle royal between the power of the hand of God and the power of Baal. Elijah boldly challenged the people of Israel:

...How long halt ye between two opinions? if the Lord be God, follow Him: but if Baal, then follow him. And the people answered him not a word (1 Kings 18:21).

The people refused to take a stand that day—and that's not good. Anytime we refuse to stand for something, we stand for nothing...and give the devil an open invitation to come on in and set up business. It's dangerous to turn our backs on what's right and do nothing. It's dangerous not to speak out against abortion, even though we secretly believe it's wrong in our hearts. It's dangerous not to protest the wrong things that we see going on around us. It's dangerous to look the other way while crime runs rampant and sin threatens to completely take over the world. When we look the other way, we think we're not taking a stand—when in fact, we are taking a stand all right, a stand for evil. We're serving Baals.

On top of Mount Carmel that day so long ago, the prophet Elijah arranged an elaborate test to see whose god was really God. He went through various sacrificial ceremonies to prepare several bullocks on an altar. Then he invited the prophets of Baal to call upon their idol-gods to send fire from heaven and consume the sacrifice.

And call ye on the name of your gods, and I will call on the name of the Lord: and the God that answereth by fire, let him be God. And all the people answered and said, It is well spoken (1 Kings 18:24).

Because Elijah's trust was in the Lord, he had no qualms whatsoever about staging such a contest. He knew his God was a consuming fire! Picture this: Those prophets of Baal were doing a lot of chanting and dancing and ritualistic things, trying to get their powerless gods to perform a miracle so they could save face before the people of Israel. They prayed. They called upon Baal. They jumped. They shouted. They went into a frenzy, jumping on top of the altar, rolling all around, dancing, prancing, on and on. This stuff probably went on for hours...and no fire fell from heaven.

And it came to pass at noon, that Elijah mocked them, and said, Cry aloud: for he is a god; either he is talking, or he is pursuing, or he is in a journey, or peradventure he sleepeth, and must be awaked. And they cried aloud, and cut themselves after their manner with knives and lancets, till the blood gushed out upon them (1 Kings 18:27-28).

Then it was Elijah's turn.

And it came to pass, when midday was past, and they prophesied until the time of the offering of the evening sacrifice, that there was neither voice, nor any to answer, nor any that regarded. And Elijah said unto all the people, Come near unto me. And all the people came near unto him. And he repaired the altar of the Lord that was broken down. And Elijah took twelve stones, according to the number of the tribes of the sons of Jacob, unto whom the word of the Lord came, saying, Israel shall be thy name: And with the stones he built an altar in the name of the Lord: and he made a trench about the altar, as great as would contain two measures of seed. And he put the wood in order, and cut the bullock in pieces, and laid him on the wood, and said, Fill four barrels with water, and pour it on the burnt sacrifice, and on the wood. And he said, Do it the second time. And they did it the second time. And he said, Do it the third time. And they did it the third time. And the water ran round about the altar; and he filled the trench also with water (1 Kings 18:29-35).

Here was Elijah, so confident in the Lord's ability to send fire to consume the sacrifice that he made it as hard as he could for the Lord to fulfill his prayer. He dowsed the whole altar—sacrifice, wood, everything—with water. Then he filled the trench with more water. Then he prayed: "Hear me, O Lord, hear me, that this people may know that Thou art the Lord God, and that Thou hast turned their heart back again" (1 Kings 18:37).

Elijah didn't do any dancing or jumping or running around shouting that day on Mount Carmel. He just prayed, then stood still...and waited for the fire to fall.

Then the fire of the Lord fell, and consumed the burnt sacrifice, and the wood, and the stones, and the dust, and licked up the water that was in the trench. And when all the people saw it, they fell on their faces: and they said, The Lord, He is the God; the Lord, He is the God (1 Kings 18:38-39).

Notice that not only did fire fall from heaven and consume the sacrifice, but it also licked the water up from the trench. Even the dust was set on fire! That's enough to blow your mind right there. God showed up so powerfully that even the dust was set on fire. The sight was so awesome that the people fell on their faces and proclaimed the winner of the contest: the Lord Most High!

No longer was there any question as to whose god was THE GOD. Without question, there was just *one God*.

Then Elijah, filled with supernatural strength by the power of the Holy Spirit, killed each one of the prophets of Baal. He pulled the strongholds down. He destroyed in a single day that with which the people of Israel had been coexisting for many years.

Called to Warfare

Yes, God's grace is sufficient, but we are called to warfare from time to time. We must exercise our God-given authority against the enemy, or he'll just keep taking charge. The devil will keep right on taking over unless we draw the line and then defend it in prayer. He'll keep right on trying to destroy our families; he'll keep right on trying to captivate our nation; he'll keep right on tearing up our communities—unless we, the called of God, take a stand and pull down the strongholds of Baal.

We can start by putting some Christian people in office. We can start by appointing some Christian policemen. We can start by supporting these individuals in their efforts to lead. We can start by taking a stand against evil—a stand for good!

If we are ever to rid our land of the famine that is upon us, if we are ever to see our families and communities restored, then we who are called of God must take a stand in the name of Jesus. We will have to pull down some strongholds. We will have to do some spiritual warfare.

There is a mentality of Baal among those in the church today, and we must not allow the Baal mentality to coexist in our midst. If people don't have the mind of Christ, and if they are not willing to conform to the things of God, then they don't belong in the house of God. Get them out of there, because to allow them to co-exist with you will destroy what God is trying to do. We must pull down the Baals. We must get rid of liars, idol worshipers, and followers of other gods. Then there will be rain for the dry land. Then the people will begin to see the hand of the Lord.

Watch what happened after Elijah dealt properly with the Baals:

And Elijah said unto Ahab, Get thee up, eat and drink; for there is a sound of abundance of rain. So Ahab went up to eat and to drink. And Elijah went up to the top of Carmel; and he cast himself down upon the earth, and put his face between his knees, and said to his servant, Go up now, look toward the sea. And he went up, and looked, and said, There is nothing. And he said, Go again seven times. And it came to pass at the seventh time, that he said, Behold, there ariseth a little cloud out of the sea, like a man's hand. And he said, Go up, say unto Ahab, Prepare thy chariot, and get thee down, that the rain stop thee not. And it came to pass in the mean while, that the heaven was black with clouds and wind, and there was a great rain... (1 Kings 18:41-45).

What caused that torrent of rain to be released upon a land previously in drought and famine? The hand of God! Once the strongholds were pulled down—once the land was rid of Baals—the rains came.

Take a bold stand for God and then look for the rain clouds—rain to refresh your dry and brittle marriage; rain to resurrect the ashes of your dying business; rain to restore your relationships with your children. Where is it that you need rain to fall on your areas of famine? Take a bold stand for God. Then stand back and watch what happens! Soon you will see the hand of God!

The hand of the Lord is your source of victory. Wherever the hand of the Lord is, there you will find liberty. God wants to control your life. He wants to control your circumstances. But in order for Him to be in control, you will have to pull down the Baals. God won't rush in and knock them over for you; you have to identify them and pull them down for yourself.

Then the Lord will refresh you and revive you and send rain on your dry ground. Submit today to the Lord and, instead of His judgment, you will see victory. You will see power. You will see the hand of God.

8

God's Hand of Guidance

S o many people today are in search of direction. The choices are endless as to which way to proceed; but there is only one right way. What is it? Only God knows: He is our Guide. We receive divine guidance by God's hand of guidance.

Guidance is another of the Lord's promises to His children. In Isaiah 58:11, we read:

And the Lord shall guide thee continually, and satisfy thy soul in drought, and make fat thy bones: and thou shalt be like a watered garden, and like a spring of water, whose waters fail not.

What powerful promises are contained in that Scripture verse!

I want to suggest that we should allow the Holy Spirit to be our Guide, because He knows all the answers. When we are in the midst of making critical decisions about our lives—decisions dealing with our families, our ministries, our lifestyles, our careers—we should not even try to make those decisions on our own. We should train ourselves to always seek God's guidance first, before doing anything else. God has the solution to every dilemma we are faced with. So there's no need for us to sit down with a calculator and try to figure our own way out of the problem. Seek God. He knows all the answers. In fact, His wisdom supersedes that of man.

God Is the Guide

God is our Guide. He is not a follower. If He is to guide us, then we will have to follow Him. That is the way it must be. We must understand who the Guide is. If God is the Guide, then we should not follow some marriage counselor. If God is the Guide, then we should not follow the voice of another, lesser guide. That's how we get into trouble—following the wrong guide.

Let's look at several Hebrew words that describe God as Guide. The first word is *nahah*. It means "to lead in the sense of conducting along the right path." God will never lead us down the wrong path if we are following Him. The idea conveyed by the word *nahah* is that of God as a conductor. In much the same way as an orchestra conductor leads a group of musicians, so God leads His people. The conductor knows all about the instruments; however, His primary responsibility is not to play them, but to lead as others play them. The music doesn't start until the conductor begins. He'll get the beat going and then bring the musicians in…one section at a time, right on time, perfectly. It's important for every musician to know when to tone it down in a decrescendo. It's important to know how to flow with the timing of the rhythm. It's important to play in tune. Just watch the Conductor; He'll be the Guide.

You may say, "Well, I know how to read sheet music." That's just fine, but you will still need the Conductor, the Holy Spirit, to help you apply what you already know. It's not for you to do your own thing. It's not for you to jump out there and play a solo, even though you can, when it's not your season for solo work. The Conductor will let you know when it's your time to play. Until then, stay with the group, play in tune, and keep up the beat. All it takes is for one instrument to get out of line—one musician to take his eyes off the Conductor—for the entire orchestra to fall apart. Watch the Conductor! He will guide you.

An example of the idea expressed by the word *nahah* can be found in Exodus 13:21-22:

And the Lord went before them by day in a pillar of a cloud, to lead them the way; and by night in a pillar of fire, to give them light; to go by day and night: He took not away the pillar of the cloud by day, nor the pillar of fire by night, from before the people.

God is our Guide, our Leader. When we're out of step with Him, we can throw the whole group off course. When a military troop is ordered to march, everyone must march together. We are in God's military marching band. That's *nahah*.

Then there is the Hebrew word *nahag*. *Nahag* means "God as a Shepherd." It connotes the whole idea of shepherding, which is also associated with the heart and nature of God the Father. What we must understand about God is that He has already predetermined what it is that He wants us to be. It has already been decided. It is up to us to find the right course to get there, then stay on it. To do that, we must have a Shepherd. He is our Shepherd.

So the word *nahag* shows God as a Shepherd leading us to His intended place of destiny. It becomes our responsibility to allow Him to lead us there. When God called Abraham, He said, "Abraham, take your son Isaac and offer him upon the mountain that I will show you." God was very specific about which mountain was to be used. Abraham was not free even to choose which mountaintop he would make his sacrifice upon. God chose.

People of Destiny

It is the same today as He leads us to our appointed destinies. God goes before us, preparing the way, leading us along as we are responsive to His voice, and herding us back on track when we have gone astray. And there will be times when we do go astray, but He is faithful to find us and direct us back on course.

Again, there is the metaphor of the sheep. We like to think we're too intelligent to be compared to sheep, which are known to be quite dumb. But we see the sheep metaphor again and again as we humans are compared to sheep in need of a Shepherd. At times sheep go astray. That's why they need shepherds—to get them back into the fold, where there is safety and provision. At times God can get us there with just the sound of His voice. At other times, when we get into trouble and stray away, it will require more severe measures. But because He loves us, the Shepherd of our souls seeks us and finds us and guides us back to safety.

When we have gone astray, we are more vulnerable to the attacks of the enemy. That's why we must allow God to always be out there in front of us, guiding, protecting, and leading us in the direction we should go. We should not rely on our own understanding to get us there; we should rely only on Him. Psalm 23 says it beautifully: "The Lord is my shepherd; I shall not want" (Ps. 23:1). That sums it up.

The Lord is *nahag*—the Shepherd, the One who guides, leads, protects, and fights our battles. He is the Greater One, our Big Brother, our Friend. He is all-powerful.

He is also *Nahal*. This Hebrew word means "to lead with care." God is caring, *nahal*. Isaiah 40:11 says: "He shall feed His flock like a shepherd: He shall gather the lambs with His arm, and carry them in His bosom, and shall gently lead those that are with young."

God is gentle. He is a caring, compassionate God, and we need to know that He cares for us because He is our Guide. He guides us by what He says, not what He sees: "For we walk by faith, not by sight" (2 Cor. 5:7).

So there will come times when our faith must be blind faith. In those times, more than any other, we must follow God purely on the basis of trust. We must follow along blindly, by faith, while He guides us to the expected destination.

Do things look especially bad right now? Seek God. Follow Him. Stop seeing. Start believing. Start trusting God, and regardless of what you see, call it what God says. Do you see sickness? Call it healing. Do you see lack? Call it plenty. He's your Guide, and He will guide you continually.

The word *nahal* means "to be done without measure; regularly, without interruption." In essence, there is nothing that should interrupt the guidance of God in the life of a believer. Let's look at Numbers 9:16: "So it was alway: the cloud covered it by day, and the appearance of fire by night." Day in, day out, there was guidance for the wandering Israelites. By day it was a cloud; by night, a pillar of fire. Day in, day out, God did not forsake His people. He guided them on a 40-year trek through the wilderness, culminated in their entrance into the promised land.

God is the same God today. He will guide you with uninterrupted guidance.

Things That Hinder

Now, the believer's progress is often paralyzed due to satanic interference and secular interruptions. But God's guidance is constant and always available. We may cease from seeking that which is divine and spiritual in order to go after that which is secular and scientific— even that which is occult and off-limits, such as astrology and other paganistic practices. God clearly warns against these things.

In Deuteronomy, chapter 18, we see God's warning to the Israelites if they chose not to follow Him: They would receive curses and not blessings, even though the blessings had been first offered to them by the hand of God.

It's the same today: Curses follow involvement in the things God hates, such as dealing with pyschics, astrology, palmistry, or paganistic practices. Believers don't have any business picking up the phone and dialing some psychic to find out if they're going to have a great day, for the Word of God says, "This is the day which the Lord hath made; we will rejoice and be glad in it" (Ps. 118:24). We don't have any business reading some book on self-esteem written by a nonbeliever when the Word of God says we are "fearfully and wonderfully made" and so valuable to God that He sent His only Son to die on Calvary for our sins (see Ps. 139:14; Jn. 3:16). What better reason to feel good about ourselves than that?

We don't need some psychoanalyst to tell us, "Be encouraged!" God says that much in His Word. He put us above the angels. Yet believers are running around, saying, "What's your sign? Mine's Scorpio!" Stop it! Put that stuff down! You're a child of God! He says, "When thou art come into the land which the Lord thy God giveth thee, thou shalt not learn to do after the abominations of those nations" (Deut. 18:9).

When you come into the land of promise—when you're where God wants you to be, standing in the midst of blessings—don't you dare conform to the standards of the world! You're above that. You're not the tail; you're the head (see Deut. 28:13). You're somebody in the sight of God.

> *There shall not be found among you any one that maketh his son or his daughter to pass through the fire, or that useth divination, or an observer of times, or an enchanter, or a witch, or a charmer, or a consulter with familiar spirits, or a wizard, or a necromancer. For all that do these things are an abomination unto the Lord: and because of these abominations the Lord thy God doth drive them out from before thee* (Deuteronomy 18:10-12).

Studying witchcraft? Big mistake! First of all, if you're covered by the blood of Jesus, that "mojo" stuff isn't going to work against you. Second, the Bible warns against it, and God calls it cursed. If you want to be blessed, have nothing to do with witchcraft, or with people who claim to be involved in those occult things. That stuff is not of God. Leave it alone.

God Who Satisfies

Not only is God our Guide; He also satisfies our souls. Let's look at Psalm 104.

> *He makes springs pour water into the ravines; it flows between the mountains. They give water to all the beasts of the field; the wild donkeys quench their thirst. The birds of the air nest by the waters; they sing among the branches. He waters the mountains from His upper chambers; the earth is satisfied by the fruit of His work.*

He makes grass grow for the cattle, and plants for man to cultivate–bringing forth food from the earth: wine that gladdens the heart of man.... The trees of the Lord are well watered, the cedars of Lebanon that He planted. There the birds make their nests; the stork has its home in the pine trees. The high mountains belong to the wild goats; the crags are a refuge for the coneys. The moon marks off the seasons, and the sun knows when to go down. You bring darkness, it becomes night, and all the beasts of the forest prowl. The lions roar for their prey and seek their food from God. The sun rises, and they steal away; they return and lie down in their dens. Then man goes out to his work, to his labor until evening. How many are your works, O Lord! In wisdom You made them all; the earth is full of Your creatures. There is the sea, vast and spacious, teeming with creatures beyond number–living things both large and small. There the ships go to and fro, and the leviathan, which you formed to frolic there. These all look to You to give them their food at the proper time. When You give it to them, they gather it up; when You open Your hand, they are satisfied with good things. When You hide Your face, they are terrified; when You take away their breath, they die and return to the dust. When You send Your Spirit, they are created, and You renew the face of the earth. May the glory of the Lord endure forever; may the Lord rejoice in His works (Psalm 104:10-31 NIV).

God is moved to satisfy. He satisfies Himself, and rejoices in His own work. Did you see that in verse 31? Whenever you see the phrase "shall be filled" in the Bible, it means "shall be satisfied." God says over and over again that His children shall be satisfied. If you're not satisfied, start seeking Him more earnestly, for He has promised to satisfy you. He'll give you joy unspeakable. He'll give you peace that will pass all understanding. He'll gratify you. Let Him be your Guide, and He will guide you into all these things that satisfy.

There is power and satisfaction in simply knowing God...and even more, in knowing God's hand of guidance.

9

God's Hand of Assurance

U.S. currency carries the time-honored phrase, "In God We Trust." What does that mean, really? Do we? Trust Him, that is. We argue about the right to pray publicly, then appoint a chaplain of the Senate. Yet nobody stands up in Congress and says, "Wait a minute! Let's ask God before we vote on that bill!" Our money says we trust God, yet there are things contradicting that assertion going on everywhere around us in our nation. To trust God means a whole lot more than simply stamping a statement to that effect on the face of our money. To trust God means to rely on Him and to lean heavily upon Him—just Him. To trust Him is to rest confidently beneath the hand of God's assurance, knowing that everything is going to be all right.

King Solomon was a man of great wisdom and stature. As writer of the Book of Proverbs, Solomon said, "Trust in the Lord with all thine heart; and lean not unto thine own understanding. In all thy ways acknowledge

Him, and He shall direct thy paths" (Prov. 3:5-6). Solomon was speaking of divine dependence, about making an investment in dependence on God. To trust means to invest in. That's what Solomon was saying: "Invest in God! Trust in the Lord wholeheartedly! Trust Him!"

Trusting in God does not mean trusting Him to answer your prayers just the way you want them answered. Trust is not saying, "Lord, I'll trust You if You'll just do such and such." Trust is saying, "Lord, not my will but Thine be done, any way You want to do it. I trust You."

Many of us have our own agendas with God. We want what we want, when we want it. But God doesn't operate like that. He has an agenda that supersedes any agenda of ours. He knows what's best, and that is what He'll do.

Sometimes this will mean we'll have to go to the cross with those things we want so badly. If it's in the Bible we can have it. Or can we? If it's not God's will for us to have it, we can't. Those are the things we must take to the cross. Jesus didn't want to go there either. He said, "Take this bitter cup from Me…" as He agonized in the garden of Gethsemane the night He was arrested. Then He said, "Nevertheless, not My will but Thine be done." (See Mark 14:36.) That settled it. He was saying, "If God is ready for Me to die, I'll die!" That's trusting in God with all thine heart.

With All Thine Heart…

The Hebrew word for *heart* does not mean the actual physical organ; rather, it refers to the emotions. Moreover, it also often relates to intellect, understanding, reflection, discernment, and the human will. So to trust in the Lord with all one's heart means to trust Him with one's will.

We are to willfully, purposefully trust God. We are to trust Him with our free will. We are to place that free will in His hands and let Him do with it as He pleases, for He knows what is best for us, and we do not.

Those in search of a mate will testify that they want someone who is good-looking, first and foremost. Women want men who are tall, dark, and handsome. Men want women who are cute, petite, slim, with long, beautiful hair. But God sees beyond all those outward things and knows exactly who is right for whom.

Maybe he's not six feet tall, and maybe he's pudgy and going bald. God sees beyond those things and into his heart. Maybe she's not petite, but is overweight and has short-cropped hair; but her heart is holy and filled with vision and God sees that she's the right one for you. What then? To trust God is a whole lot like a blind date. You're saying, "God, You choose the place and I'll show up. You choose the person and I'll take it from there. I'll trust Your choice." That's blind faith. That's trust. That's investing in God. He won't lead us astray. He won't abuse us. He won't let us down. Total dependence on Him—that's God's best for us.

In these verses from the Book of Proverbs, King Solomon is saying, "Invest your will into the will of God. Trust Him with all your heart, and He will direct your path. Don't lean on your own understanding. Don't rely on your own intellect. Trust God!" Now, if you'll be honest, you'll admit that you can't always be trusted. You know the kind of person you really are; the one God knows. You know you can't always be relied on. You know you take the easy way out sometimes. God knows too. You know you're subject to changing horses in the middle of the stream. You know you're emotional and moody and swing one way one day and another way the next. Sure, God knows it. So Solomon is saying, "Don't trust that. Don't trust yourself; trust God. He's not that way: He's reliable. He's dependable. He'll hold you steady."

There are certain things you just can't lean on. Some things, you can't rely on for any type of support—the human intellect, for instance. Did you know there is a fine line between genius and insanity? Regardless of how smart a person is, his human insight is still fallible. It can waver. I don't want to trust that; I want to talk to Christ. He will always guide me correctly. I don't want to trust in human intellect and insight; I want to trust the Lord.

The devil doesn't care about psychology. He doesn't care a thing about your "hierarchy of needs." He'll wear you out with that stuff, even have you swinging from the chandelier with how smart you are, all while he drives you up a wall with worry and harassment. You may have a masters degree in psychology, but do you have peace that surpasses all understanding? Or, are you hooked on Rolaids and stay up nights because you're too keyed up with stress to sleep? The devil doesn't respect all those things, you know. He respects just one thing—the Word of God.

Stop Trying to Figure It Out!

Solomon says, "Lean not upon your own understanding." Stop trying to figure everything out. Let the hand of God's assurance come upon you as He shows you how to trust Him, how to take Him at His Word. Get out of God's business—which is to take care of You—and roll those cares over onto Him. Let Him figure everything out. Your job is to just trust Him.

Job tried to figure everything out. He tried and tried until he wore himself out, and he still didn't have all the answers. Finally, he acknowledged his lack of understanding before the Lord and received breakthrough (see Job 42). God knew it all along; Job didn't know everything, even though he may have thought he did. All the Lord wanted was for Job to see it. And when he did, his blessings were restored to him.

How are you going to figure out that kind of God— the kind of God who made light, the planets, all animal and plant life out of nothing, merely by speaking them into existence? He simply said, "Let there be..." and creation began. There is no way to figure out that kind of God. That's why you and I must stop trying to figure Him out.

Some people are experiencing problems in their lives right this minute simply because they are working overtime trying to figure God out. Instead of releasing their problems to Him and trusting Him for answers, they are picking at them, mulling them over, looking under every rock for answers on the human, natural plane of existence. God is supernatural, and often answers in ways that are beyond human comprehension. That's a real mind-blower for intellectual types who love to think they've got all the answers.

The reason those problems seem so huge is that there is not enough room inside that problem for both you and God. So step out of it; give the whole thing to Him. Then stand back and see how He will solve it. It's a lot like learning when to fight and when to step out of the ring. The same principle applies: Let go and let God. He'll trounce your enemy right before your eyes if you'll just get out of the way.

What did Elijah do while the prophets of Baal were prancing around on top of Mount Carmel? He stood back, well out of the way, and allowed them to wear themselves out and make complete fools of themselves while it became obvious to all Israel that the gods they served were powerless to send fire from heaven. Then, at the right moment, Elijah stepped up, prayed one prayer, and wham! The fire hit! Then came the rain!

That's how badly God wants to change your current situation. Whatever it is that you've been struggling with, God can change it suddenly. Just trust Him. Turn it over to Him; then get out of the way. Soon, He'll send the fire and the rain.

Acknowledge Him!

Solomon says we are to acknowledge God in all our ways. What's that mean? Trust Him! Not the doctor's report, not the job application, not the world's system, but trust God. Start trusting Him and standing on His Word;

then see what God will do. He'll send an answer that is beyond your ability to figure it out. And when He does, you'll just know it was Him. You'll just know, because of the glory. It will fill that situation. You'll just feel it—maybe right there in the middle of your doctor's examination. You'll just experience a sense of relief, and all of a sudden you'll know—God showed up! The healing you've been trusting Him for is there!

Acknowledge Him! By that, I don't mean some casual nod of recognition. To acknowledge means to see God, to recognize Him, as if to say, "I'm glad You're here, Lord!" It carries the idea of intimacy with God. Acknowledge Him when you are faced with that situation that has you so stressed out. Don't fall to pieces—acknowledge Him!

There is not a single problem facing you today that God does not have a solution to. You may be suffering today because of what you don't know about Him. Your faith, your trust in Him, is not as great as it should be because you don't know Him intimately enough. To gain trust in someone is to gain intimate knowledge of that person, knowledge you gain by spending time with him or her.

Spend time with God. Acknowledge Him. And the Bible promises, "He will direct your path." He will get out there in front of you and clear away all the obstacles. He's already out there ahead of you, getting the road ready. He's already out there preparing the answer to those problems that are pressing you. He's already out there ahead of you walking up ahead in prosperity. He's walking in healing. He's walking in success. He's already paid the price. He gave His life for you so that road could be made ready to receive you as you walked it.

So the Holy Spirit goes in front of you and prepares the way. Then you start to walk the road He's prepared, and He reminds you, "Now, there were some potholes out there, but God has already taken care of them. I know; I primed that thing and got it ready for you so you could walk smoothly."

When you get to work tomorrow, there's going to be a blessing waiting for you. Why? Because God got there first and punched the clock. He prepared it ahead of time. When you get home, that angry husband will have gotten over your dispute with the discovery that he just can't live without you. Why? Because God got there ahead of you and got through to him.

Trust God! When you learn to rely on Him, He will direct your path. He'll fix those potholes. He'll steer you around those pitfalls. He'll pave the way for you, remove your enemies, rebuke the devil for you, and get you to your destiny.

He's already made the way; now, trust Him! The hand of God's assurance will guide you and get you safely to your destination. Glory to God!

Epilogue

I trust this message has been a blessing to you as you have studied with me the different aspects of the hand of God. Would you like to experience the hand of God to a greater degree in your life? Then pray with me:

Lord, I want Your hand upon my life. I desire to know You more intimately and want to walk with You daily as You keep me by your keeping power and pour out Your mercies upon me, mercies that are new every morning. Guide me, Lord, to my place of destiny with You. Help me to grow in the knowledge of You and learn to trust You and rely on You instead of upon my own understanding. I pray You will bless me, Lord, with more of Your presence as I seek to walk holy and upright before You. In Jesus' name, I pray. Amen.

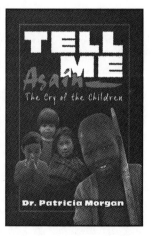